D1193461

# Burnt Toast and Jam

### Stories and Thoughts to Fill your Heart & Lift your Spirit

## D. Kinza Christenson

Peebles Publishing Unlimited
Oconomowoc, Wisconsin

Copyright © 2008 by D. Kinza Christenson

All rights reserved.

Published by
Peebles Publishing Unlimited
Oconomowoc, Wisconsin
(262) 567-6317


ISBN: 978-0-9728277-4-4


Cover design by: GB Art & Design
Typography by: The Publishing Institute


Printed in the United States.

*Dedicated to my parents*

**Bob and Frances Lathrop Peebles**

Dad, for his strength of character,
sharp wit and gentle nature
Mom, for her wisdom,
humor and embracing compassion
Together, their unconditional love and devotion
were exceeded only by
their goodness, integrity and humble dignity.

# TABLE OF CONTENTS

# FOREWORD

$C$lose your eyes. Envision a tambourine. See the colorful ribbons trailing down from the shiny metal circle that holds the stretched top. Hear the sound it makes as the dancer slowly beats the instrument against her side. Feel the pace and the sound pick up as the tambourine is shaken faster and faster. The dancer is twirling to the music and you realize you're moving, too. Maybe it's only a little movement, but the dancer, the tambourine, and the music have conspired and taken you in. There's no sense resisting—you have to participate—they've caught you.

*Burnt Toast and Jam* contains the reflections of a woman well-schooled in living a full life. From her business background, her family's adventures great and small, a long and loving marriage (well, most days loving) and life's ordinary events, Kinza Christenson recounts moments worth reviewing. With laughter and tears and poetry and prose, *Burnt Toast and Jam* will delight you.

The book you're holding in your hands is just like that tambourine you imagined. Filled with stories as colorful as the instrument's ribbons, little bits of life stretched to provide lessons in a loving way, and rhythm, always rhythm, pulling you to read just one more page. As you read, listen for the tambourine playing in the background. It will be there.

Chris Clarke-Epstein, CSP
Speaker, Trainer, Author
Past President, National Speakers Association

# PREFACE

Today, I find myself writing a book and reflecting on what has brought me to this point.

Like most people, my life has been a series of stages, experiences, friendships, choices and lessons. It's been a journey where things from the first part of my life have come full circle in the second part of life. I've learned to deal with the big things, and appreciate and savor the little things. While there has been sorrow, my heart is also full of gratitude.

My life has been a journey where I've learned to stop whining, (well, for the most part), start laughing and find the joy. Somewhere along the way, I developed the desire to help others to succeed in becoming the person he or she wants to be. Then my business background seemed to partner with my experience in the entertainment field to create the person I am today. Add to that a loving family and the incredible experience of having grandchildren, and my heart is full.

The stories and thoughts included here are intended to remind us all to:

- ♥ Affirm that we have a loving God
- ♥ Lighten up and not take ourselves too seriously
- ♥ Share love and compassion for one another
- ♥ Fill our personal reservoirs with good things
- ♥ Build a foundation to help us through the hard times

Now, I've never been the most attentive cook in the kitchen. The smell of something burning has always been a theme at our house. While guests were being welcomed at the front door, I was usually waving the smoke out the back door. One morning, when I smelled the toast burning in the kitchen, I realized it was our last piece of bread. I went to the drawer to get my knife to scrape off the burnt cinders. The toast didn't look so good but topped with sweet jam, it made my tongue curl in delight.

Then it occurred to me that so often in life, "burnt toast happens." Sometimes it's the small things that cause stress and embarrassment; sometimes it's really big things that impact our lives forever. This "burnt toast and jam" philosophy may just help to make our road a little brighter and the load a little lighter.

*Every time the toast is burnt, scrape it off, pile on that sweet jam—and find the joy in the blessings!*

*And remember, if God brings you to it,*
*He will lead you through it!*

# JUST LIFE

# Gals' Day Out

It was an excursion day, just a good friend and our two daughters. My daughter and I picked our friends up and started on our annual, two-hour journey to the Gurney Mills shopping outlet mall in northern Illinois—sure that we were in for a day of laughs and good deals as we went on our merry way.

By the time we reached the vicinity of the mall, it was close to noon, so we decided that we would pull into a Rocky Rococo's Pizza Restaurant for a bite to eat. The chattering had continued endlessly between the four of us, only stopping long enough to gasp for air. There was so much to catch up on and so little time. I guess in a fleeting thought, we might have wondered why we had to step over rolls of flooring to get to the order counter, but quite frankly, it just didn't matter.

After forming a line like good little customers, we stopped the gabbing for a moment to think about what it was that we were going to order. Quickly, we returned to sharing a few more tidbits of news and laughter. After a few minutes, we noticed there was still no one at the counter to wait on us…oh, well….and we chattered some more.

Finally, about the same time we were ready to complain about the poor service, a young man came up to us, looking strangely perplexed. Then he informed us that they were closed. We each stood in silence as we looked around the place. We were speechless. Flooring was torn up. Workmen were scurrying about in what appeared to be a blend of new construction and remodeling efforts. I could feel my face turn hot and noticed the flushed look of the other gals. Then we pulled ourselves together and indignantly huffed something about the fact they should have at least put a sign out in front saying they were closed. The workmen, by this time, had stopped working and were standing there shaking their heads and smiling at the same time as they watched us scurry out.

As we approached the car, our attention was drawn to something very large flapping in the wind above us. It was a sign bigger than life itself. I looked up and there were the words, "Closed for Business."

*The song "Fools Rush In" comes to mind.*

# THE BLACK HOLE

Have you ever wondered where exactly 'the Black Hole' can be found? I'm not sure even the scientists know for sure but I have a pretty good idea. It is in my basement. With its phenomenal sucking power, it has somehow sucked things right out from under our noses. Rest assured, however, it must be getting full. According to my rough calculations, over the years, it has sucked up an unending number of long lost socks, underwear, a check payment, a high chair tray, a wedding gift, two Christmas presents, a shoe, a vase, a pair of white slacks, a bag of chocolate chips (oops, never mind. I know where that went), several pair of earrings, at least 100 earring backings, one phone book, three pairs of reading glasses, a watch, trip directions, shopping lists and my husband's favorite shirt.

There was the time when my son was playing football in high school and I decided I would take all of his soiled socks and put them in the wash to bleach them clean. I distinctly remember taking them out of the washing machine, placing them in the clothes basket, ready for the dryer. That was the last I saw them.

Now granted I get sidetracked. I probably went upstairs and got busy with the day and probably with the next day. When I did finally remember them, they were gone. Now how does a basketful of socks disappear from the earth?

Then there was my engagement ring.

*Black holes do suck!*

# Sunrise Service

The alarm went off. Time to get up and head to church. I sang in the choir and it was the Sunrise Service for Easter Sunday. Of course, for this early service it was still dark out. I quietly scurried about getting ready in my Sunday duds, trying not to wake anyone.

I thought the choir sounded beautiful that morning as we each sang our best to herald the risen Christ. Somewhere towards the end of the sermon I looked down. Eek-k-k! Who's feet were these? Surely not mine.

There was one black shoe and there was one light brown shoe.

At the next week's choir practice, we took a break for an announcement, or so I thought. Instead, they had something else planned. They did a little skit, complete with alarm clock about the choir member who came to church with two different shoes on.

*Blessed are they who can laugh at themselves,*
*for they shall never cease to be amused.*

# LEADERSHIP 101

We were at the Milwaukee Bradley Center for a Marquette basketball game. It was a particularly thrilling night for me, as I had the distinction of being one of the opening singers for the ball game. WOW!

The next day, I told a couple of my friends about my big honor. Never knowing me to be a professional singer or in the singing industry, they were shocked. Their first response was 'How did you ever get to do that?" I just shrugged my shoulders and replied that it really wasn't hard.

That night at the game, there were the two professional singers down on the floor and then a deep, loud voice came over the loudspeaker, saying "Would you all please join in." And I did.

Now there may have been a few other people singing but I couldn't hear them. Everyone around me was chatting or too busy crunching on their popcorn, seemingly oblivious to the opportunity and duty that was before them. My heart became heavy. Flashes of bombs, funerals and grieving families flooded my mind.

As I looked around the arena that night, there were many youth there, and there were many adults. I couldn't help but think: "Where are the leaders?"

Never has there been more opportunity, or need, for leaders. Small gestures speak volumes. And, yes, the hand should be placed over the heart.

*When is the last time you led the crowd*
*in a serving of patriotic jam?*

# The Revolving Door

My daughter Darla and I were meeting our good friends, mom Dee Ann and daughter Kim, for a weekend in Chicago. Darla and I took the train to the Windy City. It was a first time for us and an exciting adventure. When we arrived at the large Chicago station, we hopped into a taxi that took us to the hotel where Dee Ann had made reservations. Now, we were not "big city" folk and at that time, a trip to Chicago was a big deal. As we pulled up to the front of the hotel, we were in awe at the majesty and formality of the doorman, who looked like he just stepped straight out of a movie. As we got out of the taxi, we glanced through the large windows of the hotel and saw our friends smiling and frantically waving hello as they watched us arrive.

I hesitated as I pondered for a moment whether my large suitcase would fit in the revolving door, but it seemed to be the most graceful way to enter. I was already half way in, so I proceeded.

All of a sudden, I heard a small voice over my shoulder, "Go Mom, go!" In her excitement, my daughter, with her own large piece of luggage, had jumped into the same revolving door slot. By the time we both realized that this probably wasn't going to work, it was too late. We were en route.

We squeezed our purses to our chests, shuffled a little, held our breath and prayed—for that split second—that we weren't going to jam the works and get stuck. Then, together, almost on cue—as if being spit out—we plummeted out of the revolving door on top of one another, stumbling over our luggage. Above us, the crystal chandeliers sparkled and around us in the elegant lobby, the bellboys, business men and stylish guests indignantly wondered what the unruly commotion was. The squeals and laughter of our friend turned into hysteric laughter as we joined them in acknowledging our grand entrance.

The scene set the tone for the entire weekend. I've often thought that if we had succumbed to the embarrassment and gotten angry, our weekend would have turned out differently. I was glad we responded the way we did. Our weekend started off on the right foot and was full of fun. We never stopped laughing.

*10% of life is what you are dealt.*
*90% is how you respond.*
—Anonymous

# A Night on the Town

There we were, two moms and two daughters, spending the weekend in Chicago to celebrate our daughters' 21st birthdays. The excitement mounted as Saturday night arrived. We went out to eat, then the girls used their new IDs and we all went into a few clubs.

We came across one rather nice pool hall attached to a club. There were other gals and couples playing at their tables. We thought it looked like fun so we decided to give it a try.

As we were setting up, a waitress came around with pretty little Jello® squares. My daughter informed me that these were "shots" and encouraged me to try one. Now usually the strongest thing I drink is Pepsi, but since this was a special night, I obliged. In between, while waiting for my turn, I might actually have had two or three. They were pretty good!

Then it was my turn up to the table. I happened to be standing at the side of the table, and could look in front of me at the long rows of pool tables lined up in front of us. As I shot my cue stick, an unexpected thing happened. My ball went airborne. It missed our table completely and headed straight toward the rows of tables filled with players. I panicked. Not sure what else to do, I yelled out very loudly "Fore"!

People ducked, stepped back and successfully got out of the way. Thank goodness no one was hurt.

Then we were politely asked to leave.

Bummer.

*Back at home, the next week I received a package in the mail. It was from my friend. Inside was a trophy of a woman with a cue stick in her hand. On the inscription it read: "Fore!"*

*Aren't friends grand? They are the "jam" of the earth.*

# The 4th of July Parade

It was always exciting when our cousins would visit us for the 4th of July. One year, we decided to have a parade from our house to Grandma's house, just down the country road a bit. We found some little horns to toot, grabbed some little flags to wave, put a leash on the goat and we were set. To Grandma's house we would go.

Years later, we lived in a small village on a lake. My kids were about the same age that I remembered us doing those 4th of July parades to Grandma's house. It occurred to me, why not have a little parade right here?

I put fliers in the neighbors mailboxes, gave a starting time and place and they would all end at my house for ice cream. Everyone was excited about it. It turned out to be one of the highlights of the summer.

It's been over thirty years now since we held the parade. As our village has grown, our parade has also grown. It now includes kids "of all ages," complete with an occasional antique car, mini-floats, decorated dogs, bikes and baby strollers. No one seems to mind that there are very few spectators. Almost everyone is in the parade —or they join in as it passes by. The parade ends at one of the homes where everyone is served ice cream.

As kids grow up and leave their village home, they take with them memories of those wonderful 4th of July parades.

*The sweetness of a good memory*
*lasts a long time.*

# BE SLOW TO CRITICIZE

Most of us are too quick to criticize. It seems to be part of human nature. Who we are and the things we do naturally seem like the right way to do things, and, therefore, we lull ourselves into thinking ours is the only way. Our actions model our habits, customs, past experiences and comfort zones. Wouldn't a much better habit be for us to learn how to bite our tongues?

With the diversity of ethnic groups increasing in our communities and in the workplace, we will be hearing and seeing many things that appear strange to us. Here is a story to help us keep everything in perspective.

A sailor one day placed a bouquet of roses on the grave of a departed comrade. As he was turning away, he saw a Chinese man placing a bowl of rice on a nearby grave. Cynically, the sailor asked, "When do you expect your dead to come and eat the rice you placed on his grave?"

The Chinese man smiled and replied: "Same time your dead friend comes back to smell the roses."

*Often our differences are exceeded only
by our similarities.*

# THE MASSAGE

One of the treats my daughter had planned during our visit was that she and I would go for a massage at a new spa in their area. Of course, the family had fun teasing me when they found out while my daughter had a girl masseuse, my appointment was with "Maurice." We were all excited when we arrived at the spa and were directed to the locker room. This was my first massage so my daughter informed me that we were to put our shoes and valuables in a locker. We were then sent to separate massage rooms.

Maurice was very nice. He introduced himself and then, for some reason oddly, excused himself from the room for a moment. I figured I was ready. I hopped up and lay down on the table.

When Maurice returned, I noted that he seemed surprised when he saw me. It then occurred to me, maybe the white robe which was hanging on the door, was meant for me. Maybe massages weren't given while you are dressed in your street clothes. I sputtered something to cover up my ignorance, telling him I had decided that he should just focus the massage on my legs since I was recovering from a knee surgery. How could I be so stupid! There was, however, no way I was going to admit it at this point.

When the massage was done, I stepped out into the hallway to meet my daughter, looking all refreshed in her nice, fluffy, white robe.

*Ignorance is not always bliss.*

# LET IT GO

*G*rowing up, my brother and sister were avid 4-H members and always spent summers grooming their show cows for the County Fair. I was perfectly happy playing dress up and looking forward to the day when maybe I could take photography in 4-H.

One spring day, my dad announced this was the year that I would be able to show at the County Fair. I was less than thrilled. My dad sensed my hesitation, but kept trying to convince me it would be okay and I could do it. Finally, he said it would be simple. We would just put a halter on one of the young calves, and I could practice leading her around the yard.

Now, in leading a calf properly, you stand on the left side of the animal, put your right had firmly on the rope just under the calf's chin and hold the rest of the rope in your left hand. I followed directions perfectly. She was a cute little black and white Holstein I named Susie. I started to walk, hopeful that Susie would follow. But she didn't move. She just stood there, her legs braced in defiance. Susie had a mind of her own and she wasn't going anywhere. I pulled and pulled, trying to encourage the cute spotted Holstein calf to walk with me. ("C'mon, please, Susie!")

Then all of a sudden, perhaps a bee stung her or something, she lunged forward and took off. ("Hey, slow down!") I soon realized I was not the one doing the leading. She was leading me. No, actually she was dragging me around the yard as I yelled and ran to stay with her and not fall down. Then it occurred to me" "All I have to do is let go of the rope."

I think stress is like that. Whether it is grudges, regrets or fears. They say over 80% of what we worry about are things we have no control over. We just need to let those go.

*Some burnt toast is meant to be thrown away.*
*Is there something that you need to let go of?*

# THE SHOW MUST GO ON

When I was teaching Middle Eastern Dance classes, our dance troupe was hired for a company party at one of our local country clubs. It was the first show for many of my students. It was their debut as dancers. The women were so nervous. They looked like professional entertainers and I was so proud of them. Each had worked very hard to perfect their routines.

The first set was to be in our beautiful ethnic costumes—more like village people. A scarf dance, performed by four women, was the very first routine. The rest of the troupe positioned themselves by sitting on the floor behind the dancers and played tambourines in time with the music. The show was off to a great start. One, two, three, swing, hop—they were synchronized to perfection. One, two, three, swing, hop—all of those hours of practice were paying off. One, two, three swing, hop—oh, no! On the "hop," Pam went crashing to the floor. Her screams filled the air as she yelled, "My leg is broken!"

Horror and disbelief struck. What do we do? Well, we kept on beating our tambourines. We knew "the show must go on." The piped-in music continued; the remaining scarf dancers continued dancing, smiling and never skipping a beat—one, two, three, swing hop.

The show was going on but something had to be done. Rather loudly, I called for the injured dancer to turn around. Two of us put our tambourines down and as discreetly as possible—still sitting (Oh, what a sight that must have been!)—inch-wormed our way forward. One of us took the fallen dancer's good leg and the other took her arm. We pulled and pulled until we had dragged her off stage, where she could get medical help.

We were saddened to learn later that Pam's femur had indeed been fractured.

*In life, things bad or unexpected things happen.*
*Split-second decisions must be made.*
*For good or for bad, you just hope*
*you make the right one.*

*I suspect that it's situations like ours that have driven*
*the old theatrical good luck wish of "Break a leg" to be*
*changed to the much better, current "Take wing!"*

# SNOWMOBILING

My hubby, an avid outdoorsman, caught the snowmobiling craze. Living in Wisconsin, we have beautiful winters and he enjoys being out in the newly fallen snow and fresh air.

One day he was snowmobiling out on the lake by himself when he went through the ice. As the ice gave way underneath him, his life flashed before him. As thoughts of "this is it" went through his mind, icy water started to surround him. The theory of "don't panic" gave way to panic. He was slowly sinking into the water with his heavy snowmobile suit and boots on and thought surely that was the end.

Then he realized his machine wasn't sinking anymore. He stood up in water that was about three feet deep. Feeling grateful and a bit foolish, he crawled out.

*Sometimes we are given glimpses into*
*what could have been.*
*These are windows of warning to heed and learn from.*
*Nothing is sweeter than being*
*given a second chance at life.*

# Neighbors for Sale

It must have been my own farm upbringing, but it just seemed like we always had pets for the kids—ducks, rabbits, dogs, homing pigeons, a horse. We had some memorable moments with a flock of homing pigeons.

What started as a fun 4-H project for the kids continued into a hobby for my hubby. Homing pigeons need to be taught how to return directly to their cages, rather than flying about the yard or landing in nearby trees. Plastic milk jugs filled with little stones worked well for scaring the pigeons out of trees. The jugs can easy be tossed at the pigeons if they should tree. It encourages and trains them to retreat to their roost.

One evening at dusk, our pigeons hadn't returned home. We were watching for them when we saw them land in a tree in our neighbor's front yard. Since it was dusk, they were determined to roost there for the night. Naturally, my hubby did what any pigeon trainer would do: he got out his milk jugs of stones.

Unknown to us, our neighbor was soaking in her upstairs hot tub, relishing her privacy and quiet time. A strange noise startled her tranquility. One look out her glass atrium and she was startled to see milk jugs flying past her window and crashing into the nearby tree. She hurriedly got dressed, ran downstairs and came outside to see what was going on. It turned out to be a call to action for an adventurous spirit, and soon she and her husband added their creativity to the challenge. But neither their garden hose nor the firecrackers worked. Those pigeons were perched there for the night.

That same summer, two of our birds did not return home one evening. Several nights later, our phone rang. It was our helpful neighbor, asking if by chance we were missing a couple of our birds. It seemed she and her husband had gone upstairs to bed only to find two pigeons perched on their headboard.

*Good neighbors are not easy to find.*
*While I'm quite sure we do not fit the bill,*
*there have been days we put ours through the mill.*

*(I think I owe them a gift. How about some jam?)*

# A New Day

This is the beginning of a new day.
I have been given this day to use as I will.
I can waste it – or use it for good,
but what I do today is important because I am exchanging
a day of my life for it!

I want it to be gain and not loss;
good and not evil;
success and not failure;

In order that I shall not regret the price that
I have paid for it.

*— Dr. H. Wilson*

# CHRISTMAS EVE

Santa always came during the night for my children and presents would surround the tree when they awoke. Bedtime Christmas Eve was always an exciting time. We'd read a few stories, then "Sh-h-h. Go to sleep now so Santa can come."

I can remember when my son was young, about 2 a.m. every Christmas Eve, the reflection of a flashlight would bounce off the wall as he made his way to the living room.

He would sit and inspect the pile that Santa had left. Then he would return to bed where he could then sleep until morning.

*It's the anticipation of good things*
*that are often the best part.*
*It's the same with life.*
*Enjoy the journey.*

# THINK BEFORE YOU ACT

The car battery on my daughter's little Civic had died. Hubby was pushing it down the driveway, steering it while he walked beside the car.

I noticed it seemed to be picking up speed as it rolled faster and faster towards our new garage door. All of a sudden, hubby disappeared from view. The rear wheel had rolled over his foot, dragging him down.

Sprawled along side the car, his long 6'2" frame was now parallel with the car. He struggled to reach inside the car in an effort to stop it before it hit the brand-new garage door. With his hand on the brake, he called to me to open the passenger door and shift the car into gear to stop it, but of course, the door was locked. After much maneuvering and a very sore hip and foot, he did manage to get the car shifted so he could take his hand off the brake. The car stopped.

His pride took a hit but he saved the new garage door!

*Never give up. Persistence pays.*

# ACCOLADES

When our granddaughter, Clara Grace, was about 10 months old, she was busy trying to accomplish her crawl. We would call to her and cheer her on, clapping at every new accomplishment. With each little achievement, we would all clap and squeal, "Good girl!" Her face would light up with a beautiful smile and her little frame would bounce with excitement as if to say, "I did it! I did it!"

Then she discovered the stairs. She loved climbing the stairs and soon learned that they were a fun and challenging thing to do, even when no one was watching. As toddlers do when they know there is an exciting place to be, she would scurry to the stairs every opportunity she had. Many times, she would be plucked up and brought down before she went up very far. Reaching the top of the stairs appeared to be her goal. It seemed like every time she tried, she would get up a little further.

Soon, when she finally make her way to the top of the stairs, she would be tickled to look at us and start clapping, reveling in her latest achievement.

When was the last time you've applauded yourself for a job well done?

*The next time you are feeling down,*
*make a list of all of your achievements,*
*no matter how small or insignificant*
*they might have seemed at the time.*
*You'll be amazed at how far you've come.*

# The Cucumber Lesson

$O$ne day, while I was speaking to an audience on how to effectively deal with change, I was sharing the concept that so many of our perceptions are unfounded. Somehow we convince ourselves, for whatever reason, about our likes and dislikes. I shared the example that I never liked cucumbers. Then as I thought about it, I realized I had never actually tried a cucumber. I just always knew that I didn't like cucumbers.

Then one evening, we were at the home of friends of ours. She brought out a tray of hors d'oeuvres. They were rye bread with cream cheese, topped with a cucumber. We were their only guests and this was their only hors d'oeuvre. In an attempt to be very gracious, I took one. I soon found myself asking for another, and another. They were wonderful! Here I had missed a lifetime of enjoying cucumbers! (Truthfully, for the sake of making my point, this is where I probably stretched my story just a bit.)

Right after my program, we went to a large dining room where we all were served a delightful lunch, which happened to include a side salad with cucumbers. It wasn't long before I received my first cucumber passed down with regards from a woman a few seats down—since I loved them so much. Soon I was given another, and another. As the cucumbers piled up, I felt a bit embarrassed. There was no way I could eat a bare slice of cucumber, at least not without the rye bread and cream cheese.

One thought came to mind. It was an old saying I had once heard:

> *Be careful of the words you say,*
> *keep them soft (truthful) and sweet;*
> *you never know from day to day,*
> *which ones you'll have to eat.*

# BE A CHANGE SURVIVOR

We are living in changing times. Wow, is that an understatement or what?! It used to be that we just changed the oil in the car or changed our baby's diapers.

Now, a day doesn't go by without each of us being faced with something changing: new policies, new technologies, new procedures, etc. Many of us don't mind change ... as long as WE don't have to change. Well, sometimes change just isn't that easy. So we dig in our heels, complain, and feel miserable.

The truth is, the future is not what it used to be...but it's going to come anyway. We might as well get on the change train and enjoy the ride. The next time you want to resist change and throw up your arms, stop and ask yourself the following points and become a change survivor.

1. What are some of the benefits you see as a result of the proposed change?

2. What are the positive aspects? Focus on these.

3. Ask yourself what you can do to facilitate the change.

4. Be flexible and open to new ideas.

*Blessed are the flexible,*
*for they will never be bent out of shape!*
—Anonymous

# Happiness Epidemic

Can you imagine opening the morning paper to see these headlines: "Happiness Epidemic Sweeps the Globe!"?

It seems that every day, we hear more and more about threatening epidemics. Why don't we all get together and start a "Happiness Epidemic"?

Are you a happy person? First of all, if you've never thought about it, you probably are and don't need to read any further. If, however, your happiness could use a boost, perhaps this will help.

Too often, we look in all the wrong places for happiness. It is as if we expect to find it growing on a tree, and when we don't find it, our attitude plummets and we justify grumpiness.

Actually, anyone can be unhappy: it's the biggest cop-out there is! It takes no effort, thought or courage, and life just gets more difficult with every passing day.

Think of happiness this way:

♥ Happiness lies within each and every one of us. We have the choice to nurture it or not.

- ♥ We owe it to ourselves to be happy. It's much healthier for us and enables us to live life to its fullest.
- ♥ We owe it to our families to be happy. We can make the lives of loved ones and friends easier, or we can make them miserable. Love chooses "easier." It isn't really a choice, though, as our spiritual journey as human beings—I believe it's our duty.
- ♥ Complaining leads to unhappiness. Stop complaining. If you never speak it, you never claim it, and the negativity shrivels and dies. But once spoken, negativity flourishes and sprouts tentacles that reach out and destroy happiness.
- ♥ Surrender your control. Worry can destroy happiness. Turn your life over to a greater power.
- ♥ Count your blessings. Focus on all the good things in your life.

*Take time to laugh. It is the music of the soul.*
*— Irish prayer*

# WHAT IS YOUR LIFE'S MISSION?

Life—none of us are getting out of it alive! Whether a life is cut short or whether it has filled 100+ years, our mortality will prevail. The "burnt toast" factor is not that we leave this earth, but that we have not made good use of our time while we were here.

Mortality claims the lives of millions of people; it claims all of us sooner or later. I have no research statistics on this but I think most would agree that the number of those who have achieved significant immortality is a much smaller number.

Therein lies our challenge. While immortality embraces spirituality, purpose and action of magnitudinal proportions, one thing is for sure—when it comes to our own immortality, we have our work cut out for us.

Perhaps the first step on this quest of striving for immortality should be thinking about the legacy we will each leave for the next generation. What do you want to be remembered for?

Have you created your own personal "Mission Statement"? Here are two questions people in our workshops are asked to answer, and to write down those answers.

1) The purpose of my life is:

2) I will achieve that purpose through …

Something magical happens when you have a clear, concise personal mission statement. It is a commitment you make to yourself. It reduces the stress over all that "little stuff" and lets you focus on what is most important to you. A personal mission statement becomes the creed by which you live your life, and it will determine the legacy you leave for others.

*All that remains when we're gone is*
*what we have given away.*

# THE GAME OF LIFE

Have the strength to face your fear;
Have a mission in life and it all becomes so clear.
Don't sweat the small stuff.
Learn to love, laugh and cheer;
It will minimize your stress and wash away the tear.

Have the confidence to look for the good in others;
Count your blessings every day.
Keep your life's balance; and
Celebrate all the little things along the way.

Believe in yourself, and trust in others;
Believe in goodness and having fun.
And in this game we call life;
You will have won.

—D. Kinza Christenson

# WEDDED BLISS

# Opposites Attract

They say that when it comes to choosing a spouse, opposites attract. I often wondered, "Why?" Wouldn't life be much easier if we were more alike?

- ♥ He's a night person: I'm a morning person;
- ♥ He loves ball games: I love musicals;
- ♥ He is great with details; I'm awful with details;
- ♥ He completes his list of tasks; I lose my list.

A good sense of humor is like a bridge. It gets you over any troubled waters.

*In the words of A. Poole:*
*"He who laughs, lasts."*

# A Long Day Fishing

One summer day, my husband convinced me to go spring river fishing with him. Now, fishing is not my expertise but, oh well, it wouldn't hurt—just this once. Our 12-year-old son all of a sudden decided he would pass on this trip.

Once we finally launched the boat, our day began. It was understood that I wouldn't be baiting my hook so cordially, my hubby obliged. Somehow I seemed to be catching more twigs than fish. Now, there was something about the right way to put an anchor in so we didn't wind up floating into the other boats and their lines. (Apparently I didn't completely grasp the technique.) And, I never could quite figure out how to untangle my line. It turned out to be a long day. To top it off, Don's favorite hat blew out of the boat and was snatched by the current. Finally we started heading for the launch. My heart leaped.

When we were getting the boat on the trailer, a rather frazzled hubby called out to "Put the minnow bucket in the back seat of the car," he didn't tell me to empty out most of the water first. He didn't tell me to set it on the floor of the backseat. As we drove away from the launch, we had to go up a rather big hill. The minnow bucket tipped over, making our back seat a swimming pool for minnows.

I don't remember much conversation on the ride home.

When we were unloading the car, our son came out. He had a funny smile on his face. (For the first time I realized why he didn't choose to come along.) Then he told his dad "I told you so."

*No one is good at everything. Everyone is good at some things. Fishing just isn't on my list!*

# THE PRIMARY REASON FOR DIVORCE

The studies are in. Of course, they substantiate what most of us already know. The main reason most people get a divorce? Marriage.

Men and women just think differently. For example, the woman who got a divorce because her husband thought he was God; she didn't.

Then there's the husband who told his wife their account was overdrawn, she said "How can that be? There are still checks in the checkbook."

Think of the differences:

- Women get PMS; men get new golf clubs.
- Women share directions for everything; men would rather die lost than ask for directions.
- Guys leave the lids up in the dark at night; having trusting hearts, women don't look.
- Women yearn for comfort and understanding; men yearn for the remote.

Then there is the man who bought his wife a shiny, beautiful new car. After spending the day in town, she called home and told him there was water in the carburetor. He asked, "Where is the car now?"

She replied: "In the lake."

While we joke a lot about marriage and our differences, it is often those initial differences that attracted us to one another in the first place. We choose spouses whose strengths complement our shortcomings. According to John Gottman, a marriage researcher (www.Gottman.com), most successful marriages make time to include the following practices:

- ♥ In the morning, they find out one thing the other is going to be doing that day.
- ♥ At the end of the workday, they have a low-stress reunion conversation.
- ♥ A daily touch, holding, kissing is done with tenderness and forgiveness.
- ♥ They schedule a weekly date for just the two of them.
- ♥ They express appreciation and admiration every day.

*We strengthen our weaknesses with the strengths of the people we choose.*

# TRICK OR TREAT

As a young married couple, our friends lived upstairs in an old house remodeled into an upstairs apartment. (My friend told me that on windy days, their toilet had waves in it.) One Halloween, she thought she'd have some fun and surprise her husband. During the day, she had strategically placed their big outside ladder up to her bathroom window.

During their meal that evening, she excused herself and went into the bathroom. There she removed her clothing, and with a tube of lipstick and watching in the mirror, meticulously, wrote "Trick or Treat" across her front, put on a raincoat, climbed out the window and proceed down the ladder. From there she went upstairs and rang the doorbell.

Her husband got up to answer the door. You can imagine his surprise when he opened the door as his wife flung open her coat. There she was in her birthday suit. Then he burst out laughing—all the words were spelled backwards.

*Good intentions count for a lot.*

---

# "HOLY, HOLY, HOLY"

The day my husband retired, he moved his suits to the back of the closet. There they remained untouched for a couple of years.

Then one day, we had to go to the funeral of a friend of ours. Hubby knew just which suit still fit him and assured me he was all set. Figuring he would just go to his closet and get dressed, he was a little short on the time he had allowed for getting ready. After an emergency pant pressing, he got dressed, remembered how to tie his tie, and we were ready. He was taking one last glance in the mirror when he noticed a little, light-colored spot on his dark pants. In another glance, he saw one or two more. He tried to flick to flick them off, to no avail.

Then he discovered they weren't spots. The light-colored spots he saw were his flesh. ("C'mon, we're going to be late"....) Upon closer scrutiny we could see that a very hungry moth had eaten multiple holes, which now jumped out at us like flashlights.

("We really need to leave, NOW...") A quick solution came to mind, that those being dark pants, perhaps we could just stick some black electrical tape on the inside of his pants, enough to cover each hole. It would be the quickest solution. We did. And it worked fine. Soon we were sitting in the church pew, the service had begun and no one suspected a thing.

The sight to behold occurred when my husband removed his pants that night. He had long since forgotten about the electrical tape, which had jumped ship from the fabric to adhere to the hair on his legs. There he was, his white briefs and his long legs covered with little black patches of electrical tape everywhere.

*When in crises, forget your pride. If it works, do it!*

# Marital Bliss

Marital Bliss. How would you define that term? I expect every person has a different definition. Then there are my husband and I. It's been said opposites attract, they are right—we did, and we are!

In our situation, my husband is the perfectionist and detailed, organized person—every woman's dream right? I, on the other hand, am more easygoing and laid back. If there's a goober of toothpaste left in the sink, I know it must be mine. He would never leave such a thing! Details are very important to my husband. He's the kind of a person who will go to the refrigerator for a treat at night, and end up straightening and cleaning out the refrigerator. Now, when most women clean the refrigerator, they take those green moldy items and throw them out. What does my husband do? He lines them up neatly on the counter. That way when I come into the kitchen, there they are— like badges to his perfection. Or are they evidence of my imperfection?

When we first married, we painted the exterior of our home, each of us doing a section. I thought this was going to be such fun. Just think of it, us working like a real 'team'! The next morning I was busy working in the house for a while and when I went out to see how he was doing, I couldn't find him. Then I went around the corner of the house to the section that I had painted the day before. There he was. Repainting what I had done. He said I had left streaks!

And, then there's the checkbook. Why is it, whenever there are mistakes they are always mine!

One beautiful, Wisconsin June day, I came home late in the afternoon. It was Saturday. We have a rather wide driveway. Normally we park on one side or the other. This day, my husband had gotten home before me and parked his truck, boat and trailer in the middle of the driveway. I had no choice but to park directly behind him. But I told him I was parked behind him. He said that was fine and he was going to pull the boat ahead and around to the backyard. I went into the house to start dinner.

I remember I had a huge pot of rhubarb cooking on the stove. The rhubarb was bubbling and smelled so sweet as I stirred it with my wooden spoon. As I stood there at the stove, I marveled at what a magnificent summer day it was. The smell of the freshly mowed lawns wafted through the air. With dinner time approaching, the neighborhood fell silent. It was so quiet. Only the rhubarb bubbled. I was reminded of how serene and truly peaceful sweet silence can be.

Then, all of a sudden, the silence was pierced by the most thunderously loud sound of scrunching, scraping steel upon steel I had ever heard! I knew what happened. I just kept on stirring. Then the silence was once again pierced. This time by what I can best describe as the wailing of a moose in labor, calling my name over and over. Now just in case, anyone in the neighborhood missed the loud steel scrunching noise, they certainly could hear these moaning wails echoing everywhere. I put my spoon down and went to have a look.

As I stood on our deck and looked toward the driveway, I saw it. It was a sight to behold. This is what I saw: There was his truck, his trailer, his boat—now this is where it got a little fuzzy. There, before my eyes was his boat motor in the windshield of my new car! Standing there, I experienced the feeling of a very warm glow go through my whole body. It felt wonderful. I hesitated for a moment, basking in the warmth and wonderment of this memorable moment.

Then, I went over to my husband. He was distraught and in a state of utter disbelief. He was almost in tears as he was exclaiming, "How could I do such thing?" He was usually so careful and calculating. How could this ever happen to him? Then he turned and looked at me and asked, "Why aren't you mad? Why aren't you yelling at me?"

I just smiled.

He didn't know it but I had just experienced true Marital Bliss!

*Isn't love grand!*

# THE WEDDING PLANS

After months of planning our daughter's wedding, I thought we had every detailed covered. The day came off beautifully. It consisted of: eight attending couples, a full church, then a pre-reception in the Church's Fellowship Hall, followed by a horse-drawn carriage ride for the bride and groom to the dinner reception. As I look back upon it, I realized I was most thankful for the little thoughts along the way that made or saved the day.

## Thought One:

Somewhere I came up with the idea to get the old song "The Chapel of Love" by the Dixie Cups. My daughter, Darla, had a five-hour drive to come home to get married. My thought: I would wake her up with this song on her wedding day. But several days before, while driving home from Minneapolis, she called me on her cell phone, delightfully squealing, "I can't believe I'm driving home to get married!" I then changed my plans for that song.

As Darla drove into the driveway, I put the tape in and turned up the volume so that the speakers on our deck rocked out as they blared "Going to the Chapel." It was a greeting she'll always remember. During the next few days, as bridesmaids and relatives arrived, they were all greeted with the Dixie Cups. It was just a little thought but it added so much fun and laughter to the anticipation of the wedding day. I couldn't help but think:

*Thank you for the thought!*

## Thought Two:

At the rehearsal dinner, everyone stood up to say a few words. With all the commotion, that was another thing I had overlooked preparing for. But somehow, I stood up and told a little story about Darla growing up. Then I did what came most natural for me. I told everyone it's a good thing to have a personal theme song, and since my daughter had gasped at the thought of having it part of the ceremony, I told them I thought it would be appropriate to do it then, in honor of the bride and groom. With laughter and hand-clapping, the entire room of guests accompanied me in my theme song: "Zippedy-do-dah"!

The next day, just as the bride and bridesmaids were dressing and preparing to leave the dressing room for the wedding procession, tears started to well up in their eyes. Their emotions were about to take over. A quick-thinking maid-of-honor remembered the song from the night before and quickly led the entourage in a chorus of "Zippedy-Do-Dah" They were then ready to go down that aisle.

*Thank you for the thought!*

## Thought Three:

I thought it would be delightful if we gave each guest a balloon and, as the bride and groom walked down the long, beautiful church steps outside, we would have a balloon lift—all letting the balloons go into the air. What a sight that would be!

Then I had the thought: I'd better call the carriage people for their input. It was there that the plan died. One balloon pop or one small breeze blowing the balloons gently onto the backs of the horses and we could have had a real catastrophe. I could see the headlines: "Bride and groom in runaway carriage catastrophe." We forgot the balloon idea.

*Thank you for the thought!*

As I look back at our event, it truly was a great day and everything went smoothly. We covered the big decisions as wedding planners recommend, but I really feel I owe the wedding's success to those special, little, unexpected thoughts.

*Good wedding planning advice:*
*Do the best you can.*
*Then relax and enjoy it...*
*oh yes, and be open to receiving those*
*special, little thoughts!*

# HAS YOUR GARDEN BEEN HOSED?

*O*ur good friends were avid gardeners. She canned, froze, and processed everything. It was an important part of their life and every meal had a serving of something freshly picked that day.

One day in early spring, they hired a man to plow under their garden to get it ready for planting. The man unloaded his machine and started to go to work. As the machine ploughed through the dirt, the worker noticed the tiller beginning to dig up something that was getting tangled in the blades. Upon closer inspection, he identified the culprit. It was pantyhose. He kept on going, uncovering pantyhose after pantyhose.

When my friend saw from her window what was happening, she did what any wife would do; she sent her husband out to deal with the situation.

As the red-faced husband sheepishly tried to help the man clean off his machine, he explained his wife had used the pantyhose last season to tie up her tomato plants.

*True love endures all.*

# THE CURE-ALL SYSTEM

Have you ever noticed that whenever you buy a new outfit, your significant other immediately comes out with "How much was it?" It's the same comment every time. Don't they see the beautiful colors, the way it fits, why you just had to have it? The fact that it was on sale and you saved a ton of money doesn't even seem to impress him. Somehow, he's always more focused on what it actually did cost, which is always too much.

I love to shop. Through my years of always yearning for the next dancing costume before I had even completed the current one, I discovered a system that carries over to those shopping mall excursions. I call it the "Cure-All System." It takes away any pain that may be involved with a purchase, the guilt that may be tugging at you or the anguish of the significant other. The best part: you get that new outfit and it even makes an honest woman of you.

This is how it works:

The next time you find that outfit you just have to have, you buy it. You take it home. You smuggle it into the house. You put in the farthest corner of your closet and let it "cure" there. How long you leave it "cure" will depend upon how expensive it was. If it was really pricey, it can involve months. Then, when the day comes that you want to wear it, you put it on. When your husband looks at you and says, "Is that new?" you can honestly look him in the eye and say: "Why no, honey, I've had this a long time."

*It's always easier to forgive the pain of the past*
*than it is to deal with pain inflicted*
*in the here and now.*

# MERRY CHRISTMAS, DEAR

There we were, arriving at the Salvation Army to help serve food one Christmas Day. It was our first time, but since we had an earlier family Christmas, my hubby and I thought it would be a good opportunity to serve and contribute the spirit of Christmas. It sparked a nice, warm feeling inside.

We were given aprons and hats and told we would be dishing up the food onto the plates in the serving line. Then we were directed to choose a station behind the large warming trays. I started to head off in a different direction when my husband caught me, saying he thought it would be nice if we worked side by side, next to each other. Now, a little red flag went up in my brain. We had been married 40 years and working side by side had never been one of our strong points. "But, hey," I thought, "It's Christmas. We can do this."

He stood in front of the sliced ham. I stood next to him, in front of the shredded turkey. The people serving the tables brought their trays of plates to us so we could fill the plates with food. They would then serve the people at the tables.

As a server, I was first in line. I soon found that it was a little tricky to figure out how much shredded turkey to put on the plates. I didn't want to over-provide, which might cause us to end up short, and I didn't want to pile so much that there was no room let for the other food. Because the turkey easily fell apart and was messy, it often took two or three attempts to get the right amount on each plate.

My husband's ham was sliced neatly and it was simply a matter of his placing the slice on the plates. It wasn't long before he suggested that he thought I wasn't putting enough turkey on the plates. (Why did this not surprise me?) I assured him that I would try to give more.

A few plates later, he instructed me that I should be doing even more. ("Yes, dear," I sighed, and found myself gritting my teeth and making every effort to comply.) Then I saw it. Still unsatisfied with the way I was doing it, he was now reaching into my turkey kettle, grabbing an extra scoop of my turkey to add to the plates before he served his ham.

Now, my husband is a task master and I realized that he was making every effort to do his assigned task and produce the best results. It is his style. It's just who he is. On most days, I can handle that. That Christmas dinner did not happen to be one of those days.

I wiped my brow, felt my blood pressure ready to boil over and found myself thinking: "Would they miss a fistful of turkey if I threw it at him?" Or, maybe I could just take this apron off and strangle him with it.

To my great relief, clarity prevailed and a simple solution popped into my head. I informed him that he had just inherited the shredded turkey in gravy. I would do the ham.

A few minutes later, I heard a sigh and the words, "Gosh, this isn't so easy."

*(Oh, really?)... Merry Christmas, dear.*

# Humble Pie

It was a cousin's lovely wedding reception. You know the routine. You primp and take pains to look your best for the celebratory event. In essence, you make every effort to put your best foot forward and make a good impression for a fun evening.

We had met many of the new relatives and I was aware of murmurs of cousins relating to their spouses the fact that they had just seen me on stage locally at one of my wellness shows. I remember feeling a glimmer of pride; for one fleeting moment, it was almost like I was a bit of a celebrity. Well, maybe at least amongst the family anyway.

The music was pounding and I loved the opportunity to get out on that dance floor. Everything was going great when the DJ announced a circle dance and got everyone up to join in. The dance floor was now crowded. We all were to take turns dancing in the middle of the circle. My turn came. Because of my dancing background, I felt the pressure was on a bit to do a good job, so I gave it my all. Twirling and jiving to the music felt so good. All eyes seemed to be on me as everyone clapped to the sound of the music.

Then, as I did my twirl to turn back to my place in line in front of the door, I could feel my foot slip out of my shoe. I found myself being propelled into orbit. My arms out and flailing to keep balanced and ahead of the momentum as I struggled to keep putting one foot under me so as not to fall.

The clapping stopped. Everyone looked helplessly on at the spectacle. I was now like a helicopter out of control. I just kept orbiting. Just inches away from slamming into the door, and ending up in a snow bank, my husband reached out and caught me in his arms—it almost knocked him over but saved me from certain demise.

Now, there's not much one can do at this point. So when I found nothing was hurting and everything seemed to be working, I made the attempt to nod that I was all right and everyone resumed the dancing ….as I swallowed my piece of humble pie.

I was reminded that humility is good for the soul.

*I also learned that humble pie*
*is not very sweet—actually it's more like burnt toast.*

# THE SECRET TO A GOOD MARRIAGE

As far as I can tell, the secret to having a good marriage is still a secret. No one I know has the magic recipe. We all have days when a little arsenic would come in handy.

The state of wedded bliss might very well be achieved with these "To Do" tips for couples:

- *A good wife always forgives her husband when she's wrong.*

- *A husband should forget his mistakes. (There's no use in two people remembering forever.)*

- *Never go to bed angry at each other; stay up and fight.* (Phyllis Diller)

Oh yes, and if I were to add one more, it would be:

♥ *Have a sense of humor—and use it. As long as you both keep laughing, there's no way you can strangle each other.*

(Now that I think of it, I wonder where that saying "died laughing" came from.)

*We ordered a case of jam today.*

# A Coaching "Oops"

My hubby coached high school basketball for years. He and his partner would travel to all the surrounding schools for games. After a long day at work, he would get home with just enough time to grab his duffle bag and clothes and he was off again.

One night he was in a particular hurry. He grabbed his things and out the door he went.

I'm told they arrived pretty much just in time to get dressed before the game was scheduled to begin. In the locker room, he hastily pulled out his black pants. His first thought: Gee, these must have shrunk. A closer look and he realized that he had grabbed a pair of my black slacks by mistake.

He's 6'2 and I'm 5'2. No, those pants were not going to work. The game was delayed until the coach got a pair of pants. One of the teachers working the game ran home and brought back a pair of borrowed pants for him to wear. Somehow I wasn't high on his list that night.

*Burnt toast, any one?*

# Our Sunset Cruise

Forty years of being married to the same person (I was a child bride) and I don't think we've ever had a dull moment. A roller coaster, up-and-down kind of happening as we found ways to bridge the differences between "Venus" and "Mars," our marriage really has been all-encompassing. Giving birth, watching the children grow and the grandchildren coming into the family, the joys, the sadness, all the heart tugs that go with marriage and raising a family. A marriage really becomes like an organizational umbrella under which all things occur and individuals are interwoven in a lifetime of experiences and events, each intricately connected with the other.

Now that our home is quieter, one of our summertime enjoyments is taking our pontoon boat out onto the lake to watch the sunset. Don and I have seen spectacular sunsets painted across ever-changing skies, with their colors reflected on the water, enveloping us in their radiance. It's as if we are in a box seat for God's majestic panoramic show. We sip our drinks, listen to Louis Armstrong's "It's a Wonderful Life," reflect on the day, and breathe in the beauty of yet another sunset. It's been a good day.

*When they asked the Reverend Billy Graham what the greatest lesson he learned in all of his years, he simply said, "The brevity of life."*

# PARENTING

# I Wish I May,
# I Wish I Might

As a little girl, our daughter Darla had never been one to ask, much less beg, for anything. She was very easy going and easily pleased.

When she was approaching her 10th birthday, she made it known that what she really wanted for her birthday were pierced ears. Of course, I was pretty adamant that she was too young for those, and thought about all the logical reasons she shouldn't have them.

One evening at bedtime, I saw her gazing out our front picture window. She had been there quite a while when I finally asked what it was she was doing. My daughter, who had never asked for anything before, replied: "I'm wishing upon a star that I might get pierced ears for my birthday."

I made the appointment the next day.

*Some things are just more about heart.*

# Bug Juice, Anyone?

One day, our neighbors were caring for their curly-haired, blue-eyed, adorable, little, 4-year old grandson, Mitchell. It was a warm summer day and they were sipping a refreshing drink. As grandmas and grandpas often do, they were discussing something very important.

Little Mitchell seemed to have something on his mind and all of a sudden he excitedly started to interrupt. Determined that this was her opportunity to teach the little squirt the lesson of the impropriety of interrupting, Grandma repeatedly told him to sit down and wait until she was done talking. After all, isn't this what grandmas are supposed to do? Frustrated, Mitchell finally sat quietly with lip quivering and a tear in his eye.

When Grandma finally finished with her conversation and her drink, she turned to little Mitchell and said, "Okay, Mitchell, we're finished. What did you want to tell me?"

In his little voice and lip quivering, he replied, "There was a bug in your drink."

*Lessons taught aren't always the lessons learned.*

# THE EASTER EGGS

When my children were both still preschoolers, they shared the same room that had a beautiful French door-like window. It was the day before Easter and I thought how fun it would be to have the kids awake Easter morning to see Easter eggs lying about the daffodils and green grass outside their window.

I was a mom with a mission, while the kids were at the neighbor's playing, I dyed and colored the eggs. That night, once the kids were tucked in and sound asleep, I put on my coat, loaded a bucket up with brightly colored eggs, grabbed a flashlight and ventured out into the night, and tucked eggs here and hid them there until each egg had been strategically placed. My mission was complete.

It was about 3 a.m. when the loud crack of thunder woke me up. Then the rain came. It pounded against the house with the brutality and fury. The downpour continued until dawn.

At 6 a.m., I bounced out of bed, scurrying to the kids' room so I could assess the situation before they awoke. I looked out the window. Everywhere I looked, ridiculous white eggs lying about like pathetic little islands in puddles of water.

I pulled the shades and went back to bed.

*I think these small disappointments happen*
*to prepare us and strengthen us to*
*handle the larger disappointments in life.*

# A Healthy Dose of Silly

All the years my kids were in high school, when they would take the car for the night, we would always call out as they were leaving, "Be careful, be good and don't speed!" We hounded and pounded those words into their minds.

Recently my daughter shared with me that whenever they were leaving her friend Heather's house, Heather's mom would lean out the door, wave and exclaim: "Be silly!"

What a contrast! After pondering this one, I came to realize this was a wonderful gift that mom gave her daughter.

Years later, her daughter has seen her mom through cancer and watched her parents as they deal with her dad's Multiple Sclerosis. The gift of laughter lightens a heavy heart and ignites better health, hope, and happiness. Wouldn't it be wonderful if we could feel silly more often?

Recently my husband was leaving to go somewhere he really didn't want to, so I leaned out the door and cheered "Be silly!" He muttered something with a bit of a groan, and then laughed. I think it must have lightened his mood that day.

> *While a dose of common sense and caution*
> *are important, don't forget to be a little silly.*
> *It does the body good and will help you*
> *through the bad times.*

# THE BIG TALK

A father spoke to his son. "'It's time we had a little talk, my son. Soon you will have urges and feelings you've never had before. Your heart will pound and your hands will sweat. You'll be preoccupied and won't be able to think of anything else."

The boy stared wide eyed and said, "Yes."

The father continued, "But don't worry, it's perfectly normal. It's called golf."

*Happy parenting!*

# A Point of Light

This young generation of girls and boys that we see,
　　　has been proclaimed the next Great Generation to be.
Oh, watch their potential soar and their goodness decree,
　　　if this prophecy is to be fulfilled, it is up to you and to me.

There is a point when you cannot walk away,
　　　when you must stand up, and mean the words you say.
There is a point you must decide, just to do it because it's right,
　　　that's when you become a point of light.

Our children need leaders to help them grow true and strong;
　　　to live with dignity and honor, knowing right from wrong.
All it takes is a point of light, a ray of hope in a dark night,
　　　someone to plan the seeds that will one day come to ripe.

What is your mission, what is your song?
　　　Remember this, as you ponder what part you will play;
All that remains of you once you are gone,
　　　is that which you have given away.

One by one, from each child we see,
　　　Beckoning for appoint of light from you and from me.
So let your light shine, lead the way, play a part;
　　　The making of the next Great Generation has had its start.

—Randy Travis song lyrics,
adapted by D. Kinza Christenson

# MAKING POINTS

This was another week of blissfully fulfilling our role as grandparents. Ethan and Maxwell were coming to visit. As a grandmother I was thrilled, yet took this opportunity very seriously. Since we don't have a chance to see them often, this was my chance to squeeze, hug, and play and, along the way, make some points for teaching good things, instilling the importance of obeying, respecting and– you know the list.

A horrendous storm hit on the first day of their visit. Living on the lake, the wind and torrential rains tore up trees and piers and we were thankful to have saved our boat. Then we discovered that our car somehow managed to get its floor flooded while it was parked in the driveway during the storm. It was a hectic and frantic day.

Two days, later we loaded the kids in the SUV and drove to the garage to pick up the dried-out and repaired car. We dropped my husband off. I again loaded the chattering, happy kids into the SUV, seat belts fastened, shoes tied, treats opened and toys in hand The boys were ready to go ---Whew! I hopped in the front seat and we were off. I decided to take the shorter, newly constructed bypass route to our house.

I had apparently been driving quite a while before I noticed a flickering in the rearview mirror. What could that annoying light be? (I had apparently overlooked adjusting the mirror when I hopped into the car.) Yep, there it was. A police car was chasing Grandma.

I pulled over, swallowed hard and rolled down my window. Apparently, the old 55-mph road was now 35 mph. and, yes, he had been behind me for quite a while. As the policeman wrote out the ticket; I noticed the boys were, for the first time, silent. As we drove home, I heard the oldest whisper to the younger something about Grandma breaking the law. I then made a rather feeble attempt to explain that all drivers have to obey the law and that somehow Grandma just didn't realize she was going that fast. Then I changed the subject. End of topic. The kids were quiet. Feeling good that I had at least squelched any lingering thoughts of the incident in the kids' minds, we continued the short drive home.

As soon as they were out of the car, they raced to find Grandpa, yelling at the top of their lungs, "Grandma got arrested!"

A few days later, we began the 5-hour ride to their homes in Minneapolis—it seemed longer than usual. Every time we saw a police car, little voices in the back seat blurted out that curious question: "Grandma, are we going to get arrested again?"

Grandma made points that week, but not the kind she intended. So much for that list of being an influence of doing good things, obeying and being respectful.

*Anybody smell toast burning?*

# "An Elephant on My Chest"

When he was two years old, our son David was diagnosed with chronic asthma. When asthma struck, he struggled to breathe, chest heaving with the effort. Soon he would be too sick to even whimper. In those days, they didn't have breathing machines for patients at home. We soon learned to be proficient at taking his pulse, and checking during the night to make certain his lips weren't turning purple. Once it reached that stage, off we'd go to the emergency room. It usually meant a good week or more in the hospital oxygen tent. He looked so frail and little as he lay there.

The hospital was a lonely place for him. We would stay there with him but there's something about an oxygen tent that is very isolating. He kept his favorite little tiger close, and the waiting game would begin. "Oh, please God, let him be okay." How often we prayed that prayer.

One night, when he was sick at home, we didn't realize he had gotten so sick during the night. When we awoke and checked, his little body was limp, almost lifeless. Terror clutched my heart as we sped him into the hospital. "Oh please, please, please, God, let him be okay." That particular attack was especially bad, and David almost didn't make it through that next night. They told us, as if preparing for the worst, that had he been born a girl, his chances would have been much better. For some reason boys had higher fatality rates from asthma. We just kept praying. Morning broke. David opened his eyes. We sighed with relief. "Thank you, God."

As he got older, I learned that one simple, seemingly insignificant cough during the day was the sign that an episode was rapidly approaching. Within hours, he would be lying on the couch, his little body quivering from the medicine. And we would begin a long, two-week siege of recovery: the medicine, the constant watch, the worry, and the prayer.

I remember when the bus came to pick him up for his first day of school. While other moms were grinning with joy that their kids were finally going to school, I had tears running down my cheeks. They were tears of relief from the many times we spent wondering if he would ever see this day.

We learned to plan things, but never count on them happening. Spring, winter and fall held sure promise of bouts with acute asthma. David would be so thrilled at the Halloween costumes I made him each year, only to never have the chance to wear them. There were overnights that didn't happen, birthday parties and Boy Scout trips he had to miss. One of the first autumns David was healthy—he must have been about 12—he got off the school bus and burst into the kitchen, asking me if I had seen how beautiful the leaves were on the trees. It was as if he had seen the autumn leaves in all their glory for the very first time.

*Praise be to God.*

When David was about 22 years old, we wrote and illustrated a book for other kids with asthma, called "An Elephant on My Chest."

# THE HAIR CUT

When does giving advice to your children ever sink in? Most of the time they completely ignore it, grabbing a cookie and running out the door—or they take offense to it and they respond in anger at your audacity. Do either of these scenarios sound familiar?

When they were young, I always gave my kids their hair cuts. It was usually a fun, sharing time. I had set the ground rules from early on that hair cut time was to be a happy time—I would accept no "flack." As they grew into teens, my daughter's longer hair required more shaping knowledge and finesse and thus, she was sent to the beauty salon for her cuts. However, I was fortunate enough to have a teen son who still thought I gave the best hair cut in town.

A hair cut? Oh no. It was much more. I found that as the days went by during the week, I would prioritize the things that I felt needed to be spoken about—if I had a vital point to make—I saved it for the "hair cut." My son's hair style at the time was one where I would use a hair pick to hold the length of the hair I was cutting an "inth degree" away from his scalp and run the shaver across the top. It worked beautifully. My son also knew if he so much as flinched he could end up with a bald spot.

This was the perfect time to encourage "sharing," add a dash of humor and then, at exactly the right time—Wham, I'd slide in my profound parental advice. It really worked beautifully. I never dwelled on the subject long enough to antagonize him—but at the same time I let him know where I stood.

Think of it: I had his complete, 100% attention. He was in a very delicate position that made it too risky to give a rebuttal. As a result, he would silently endure, and just hope his hair cut would come out looking as good as it did last time.

*Things aren't always what they seem.*
*Seek what lies beyond.*

# THE IRONY OF IT ALL

You grow up and give birth.
The babies wake you up, sleepless nights.
The new puppy wakes you up; sleepless nights.
The teenagers out with the car, sleepless nights.
The old dog now gets you up; sleepless nights.

The house is quiet, the kids moved out
and the dog is now gone.
Finally a good night's sleep.
Like most good things it didn't last long.
Now with hot flashes and bathroom calls,
sleepless nights are here again.

*I think we just weren't meant to sleep.*

# THE LONE RANGER RIDES AGAIN

When my son, David, was a toddler, he would put on his cowboy hat and gallop around the house on his little stick horse. In his ever-creative mind, he was on a magnificent horse that lived and breathed and he was loving it. It seemed that he could do a perfect "whinny" even before he could talk. Every Christmas, he asked Santa for the plastic, 8-inch Lone Ranger and horse Silver toy, complete with saddle, saddle bags, halter, reins and all of the trimmings. David played hard and constant with the Lone Ranger and Silver and it seemed Christmas would come again just in time to replace the old, worn-out and broken ones.

As David became a preschooler and it was time for his favorite television show "The Lone Ranger," he would scramble to get dressed in his boots, cape, hat, holster and, of course, his black eye mask. He would then jump on his horse and with a whoop and holler, be ready to enjoy his show—not as a spectator but as an actual character in the show. Eventually he learned how to lasso things with his rope as he "rode" with the Lone Ranger.

One summer day, we were in the lake by the pier enjoying the water, when I looked up, there was David coming onto the pier, dressed in his swimming suit, black cape, hat, holster and black eye mask. He ran down the length of pier, leaped high to jump into the water and as he did so, he drew his guns high into the air, yelling "Hi Ho, Silver!" We all doubled over with laughter but it was a sight I will cherish forever.

David's love of the Lone Ranger continued through the years. I remember when he was about seven years old, someone asked him what he would like to be when he grew up, he replied, "The Lone Ranger." I cannot help but think what a great role model this television character provided for our son. He stood for all that is good, he went to the aid of people in need of help, he was respectful, fought against evil, and when it was time to be thanked by the grateful benefactors for all he had done, the Lone Ranger had already left, never taking credit for what he had done.

In college, my son lived in a little town in northern Wisconsin. He did home painting jobs to subsidize his education. Being an outdoorsman, he always enjoyed ice fishing whenever he got the chance. One Saturday, not too long after the first ice, he took his gear and headed out onto the ice to an area where he had tested the ice depth and determined it to be safe.

Other than a few elderly gentlemen also fishing not too far from him, it was pretty quiet on this clear, crisp December day. He noticed one of the older men started walking, alone, out quite far from shore Dave wondered how safe the ice would be that far out. At the same instant as his thought, the man disappeared from sight. Panic swelled within David as he realized what had happened.

The other men hadn't noticed and when Dave yelled, they just stood as if anchored by their age and bewilderment. They were motionless.

Dave's instincts took over. He dropped everything and started running off the ice back to his truck where he kept his work supplies. He grabbed his long, heavy-duty, orange extension cord. With his cord in his hands, he came running onto the ice, directing the elderly men to come and help pull.

Then, almost like a scene out of one of those Lone Ranger shows, David whirled the orange extension cord around, much like his lasso of long ago, and building momentum, shot the end of the cord into the air to span the distance to reach the sinking man. David dug his heels into the ice and pulled with all of his might. Eventually the man was pulled onto the ice, exhausted but ever so grateful.

By then, squad cars and an ambulance were on the shore. And as happens in a crisis, all attention went to the survivor. No one noticed as my son went about his business of winding up his cord and getting back into his truck.

That night on the news there was a story about a heroic rescue of an ice fisherman by a fast-thinking young man who threw the only thing he had, a long heavy-duty extension cord, to save the drowning man. My son's name, identifying him as the hero, was nowhere.

When I learned of this incident, my motherly instincts were triggered. Why hadn't they given my son credit for what he had done? Why hadn't they acknowledged who the hero was?

All of a sudden, memories came back of a little boy in his eye-mask on his jumping horse, riding hard as he whirled his lasso high into the air to come to the aid of another. I remembered how many hours this boy had trained with the best. I had to remind myself that it was okay and fitting that he not be identified, after all that's how it was supposed to be.

The radio broadcast and the headlines on that morning paper? Their titles probably should have been: "The Lone Ranger Rides Again!"

*A child grows to emulate his heroes; steer him wisely.*

# TALKING WITH YOUR KIDS

N ow we know that parents need to talk with their kids. This seems like a no-brainer to parenting. So what has changed?

I had an engagement to be the opening, keynote speaker on my "Bridging the Generational Divides" program. At the last minute, I had created a PowerPoint slide of "Millennial-eese." It contained all the most common abbreviations used in text messaging. Since the big value in this session was not only to gain greater understanding of each generation, but extended to how to emotionally connect with others using GenerVision™ , this slide seemed to fit perfectly. The attendees were intrigued, as many of them had not realized the extent of this new "language." I also shared a conversation I had experienced the night before.

I had just arrived at the lovely resort where the conference was being held. As I unloaded my car, I chatted with a man named Mike standing nearby. We exchanged niceties and when I mentioned my generation program, Mike confided that he had resisted learning how to text message, even though he knew his 14-year-old daughter was an avid TMer. But he decided to take on the challenge and about a week after learning the basics and text messaging with his daughter, Mike received this message:

"Gee, Dad, it is so nice having you talk with me."

*"We don't see things as they are;*
*we see things as we are."*
—Anaïs Nin

*To really connect with others,*
*we need to walk in their shoes.*

# Out of the
# Mouths of Babes

When he was three years old, Ethan and his dad would often watch the Twins baseball team play on television. When his folks announced they were going to take him to a Twins baseball game, he was very perplexed. He looked at the television and asked: "But how do we get in there?"

♥ ♥ ♥

Maxwell, who was about five years old at the time, was once again asking his mom for a baby sister or brother. She replied, we'll have to ask Daddy. Maxwell frowned. He didn't know what Daddy possibly had to do with it. He said, "Daddy? I'm asking God." He turned and went over to corner and with his hand up to his mouth, whispered, as if in conversation. With excitement in his eyes, he turned to his mom and exclaimed, "Mommy, he said 'YES'!"

♥ ♥ ♥

After going to Great-grandpa's funeral, Ethan became all consumed with the topic of dying. The next day, Mom answered the door. Before she could even greet the visitors, Ethan ran up exclaiming, "Daddy's grandpa died. He is up with Jesus and Santa -- and I can ride a 2-wheel bike all by myself."

♥ ♥ ♥

Mary's husband had passed away several months earlier. Due to a road construction in their small town, the detour took them through the cemetery. One day she was driving home with her little grandson in the car. As they drove through the cemetery, he commented, "Grandma, we're in heaven." She asked him to explain. "Well, they said Grandpa went to heaven and this is where we put him."

♥ ♥ ♥

One day, our recently-potty-trained, preschool grandson assumed the position in front of the toilet. He proudly announced he knew how to spell the word toilet.

"Really?" his mom replied, "how?"

He confidently responded: "K-O-H-L-E-R."

♥ ♥ ♥

When she briefly stopped by the house to pick up something, it was good to see my niece, Renda, and her little girl, four-year-old Ella. Although they were there just a few minutes, Ella was quick to say she was hungry and wondered if I had any treats?

Knowing her mother was in a hurry, I told Ella we were going on a trip the next day and my cupboards were bare. I just shrugged my shoulders and told her I just had no food to give her today.

A few weeks later at their church, the minister was talking about the starving people in the world who have no food to eat. Little Ella leaned over and whispered to her mom, "Like Auntie Donna."

Thrilled with a new little alarm clock that sang his name to a peppy, little, "Wake-up, Sleepyhead" tune, his folks were delighted to see Maxwell bound out of bed, excited to brush his teeth to the endearing song. Then one night when he had his little friend over to spend the night, he was heard whispering to his friend, "Now, we can't get up. We have to stay in bed until the alarm goes off."

Little Megan often plays out in her yard. One evening, the wind was blowing in her direction and she heard a man's voice on a nearby school loudspeaker for a football game a few blocks away.

She looked up, puzzled at first, then excitedly got her mom's attention.

In awe, Megan whispered, "Mommy, God is talking to us!"

*Grandchildren are gifts of God.*
*I think it is God's way of compensating us*
*for growing old.*

# LET ME HOLD HER WHILE SHE SLEEPS

As a little girl, I loved playing with dolls. Playing house was a favorite pasttime. There was something about the mothering instinct that brought such joy, even as a young girl. When I grew up and was married, the day came when I had my own babies. They would be nurtured, changed, fed, picked up when they fell and taught new things about the world around them.

Now, as a grandmother I have discovered there is a whole new dimension to life as you hold your grandchild in your arms. All those motherly instincts that relaxed as my own children grew to adulthood, are rekindled and blossom into glory as one experiences life coming full circle.

Inspired by Allene, Nancy and Shelley, the following poem was written as an extension of the pain and sorrow I have felt for anyone with debilitative illnesses as hearts are bursting with the love and admiration of their new little one. Like in women everywhere, the heart just opens up.

My baby grew up and was married and had a baby girl;
The minute we heard the news our hearts went into a whirl.
Baby was healthy and beautiful as we heard her newborn cry,
A prayer of thanks to the Almighty we did sigh.

Her gentle breathing is as soft as an angel whisper,
So peaceful as she dreams of her wonderful life;
I stroke her hair and hold her dimpled fingers;
Will she ever know the depth of my love?
Oh, let me hold her while she sleeps.

My arms are weak, the strength isn't there;
To grasp, carry or catch – all I can do is deeply care;
I long to pick up my grandbaby as I watch her creep;
To feel her skin so soft and kiss her on her rosey cheeks,
Oh, let me hold her while she sleeps.

Months have passed and our grandbaby has grown,
From crawling to walking, this toddler has tricks she's shown.
Making discoveries, wiggly and squiggly one just can't sit still;
Full of youthful curiosities she not about to quell.

I can tell her stories of her mommy as a child;
Of puppies, merry-go-rounds and fawns in the wild.
Of life full of promises, that she can fulfill;
And all of my love for her that will last until eternity still.
Oh, let me hold her while she sleeps.

—D. Kinza Christenson

# Simple Can Be Special

We were going to have our two grandsons visit us: Maxwell who is six years old and Ethan who is three years old. I brainstormed quite a bit in preparation for their week visit from Minnesota. Where we could take them? Surely, we needed to do something very special to entertain them. Wrong.

I remembered the last time their families visited. They were amazed when they realized they had all been here four days and never went anywhere. The kids had not been in their car seats for four days, unheard of in their fast-paced world.

Now, when the kids arrived, they immediately found the two little cowboy hats. They spent hours playing cowboy, using their imaginations and creativity; and, then there were the 4-wheeler rides with Grandpa. One day, they found a tree frog. He was a delightful little tree frog whom they took turns holding. He was a beautiful green and it was so exciting to feel this little creature in the palm of their hands. They spent time picking up sticks for Grandpa, so he could mow the yard. Even that was great fun. Each ran to outdo the other and make his pile the biggest.

We played ball with neighbor kids in our front yard using Frisbees for bases and a plastic bat. I cheered like crazy when they made a hit. They were intrigued with Grandpa's fish that he caught and enjoyed the honor of Grandpa letting them sit in his fishing boat.

Then we had our cookie bake. We mixed the ingredients, baked, and decorated cookies for Ethan's little sister Clara's first birthday party. The cookies were in the shape of fish and each was a good size, decorated with creativity and care. It took a long time. They were so proud of each of their trophy cookies. They each knew just which ones they had done. We arranged the cookies carefully in boxes so they wouldn't break before getting to the upcoming party back home.

Before we knew it, it was time to pack the car and begin driving the kids home.

*Just like your stomach, a child doesn't need*
*all you can afford to give it.*
*The simple things are sometimes the best.*

# THE KINGDOM OF "MINE"

One Christmas, grandson Maxwell, then 18 months old, was with us from out of state. We hadn't seen him since Thanksgiving and were thrilled to be able to share our Christmas with him. When he saw all the presents under the tree waiting for Christmas, we discovered he had learned a new concept and a new word since we had seen him four weeks earlier.

He ran to the tree and one by one starting picking up the presents, saying "Mine" and busily took them over to his "Mine" pile. If we had something in our hands, he would look kind of troubled, come over and take it out of our hands, saying "Mine." Like a little knight, he built a stockpile of "Mine," I'm sure in his mind he was guarding his throne. Thrilled to see him entering into a whole new phase of development, we watched with delight at these precious moments.

As I thought about this the next day, it came to me that while we consider that a normal "phase" of childhood. I think many of us never completely grow out of it when we become adults. It is assumed that we know the fine line between the importance of taking care of "Mine" and the contrasting concept that everything exists for the sake of "Mine." But that isn't always the case.

Think of it. Aren't we as adults still tempted to become knights of the Kingdom of Mine: hesitant to let go, hesitant to share, reluctant to give credit to others, and quick to hoard. Why do many foreign nations resent Americans? They see us as living in a "Mine" Syndrome society.

The people whom most of us tend to admire are those who have gotten past this "Mine" phase and think in terms of others rather than themselves. They have left their toddler "Kingdom of Mine-hood" for the more precious treasurers of life. I know the next time I find myself caught in the "Mine" Syndrome, I need to take a moment to think of the toddler and make certain the doors of that little kingdom are closed behind me forever.

*Once upon a time there was a Kingdom of "Mine,"*
*everything I touched, I owned—even the time;*
*then I grew older and wiser and things all fell into line,*

*I realized I was but a speck in a universe ever so sublime*
*a place where souls were meant to share*
*and help others to climb;*
*where love and reason reign, and hearts were meant to be kind.*

*—D. Kinza Chrstenson*

# THE DINNER

John invited his mother over for dinner. During the meal, his mother couldn't help noticing how beautiful John's roommate was. She had long been suspicious of a relationship between John and his roommate and this made her more curious.

Over the course of the evening, while watching the two interact, she started to wonder if there was more between John and the roommate than met the eye.

Reading his mom's thoughts, John volunteered, "I know what you must be thinking, but I assure you, Julie and I are just roommates."

About a week later, Julie came to John and said, "Ever since your mother came to dinner, I've been unable to find the beautiful, silver gravy ladle. You don't suppose she took it, do you? John said, "Well, I doubt it, but I'll write her a letter just to be sure. So he sat down and wrote:

*Dear Mother,*
*I'm not saying you "did" take the gravy ladle from*
*my house, and I'm not saying you "did not" take*

*the ladle. But the fact remains that one has been missing ever since you were here for dinner."*
*Love, John*

Several days later, John received a letter from his mother, which read:

*Dear Son,*
*I'm not saying that you "do" sleep with Julie, and I'm not saying that you "do not" sleep with Julie. But the fact remains that if she was sleeping in her own bed, she should have found the gravy ladle by now.*
*Love, Mom*

*Burnt Toast Rule #1: Never lie to your mother.*

# WOMANHOOD

# BE YOUR OWN CHEERLEADER

Staying healthy and keeping the weight factor in check has always been a struggle for me. I have a tummy that is like a mushroom waiting to explode. I used to call it my curse, now it's my "blessing," and you know what they say about blessings: as you age, your blessings increase (and it does!) When trying to drop those extra pounds, it always helps me to visualize my little guards in my head. As long as they are on duty, making me stay on top of my game and think about my choices, I'm fine. When they start slacking off, I need to grind the motivation gears and set things straight again.

Football teams have known for years the value that cheerleaders have in motivating them to make those touchdowns. Mary McBride, writer for Joan Rivers, came up with some personal cheers. I've included a few of them in the collection of "Cheers" that help me get those little soldiers in my head to stand at attention:

♥ Nothing tastes as good as being thin feels

- ♥ Bakery bags make saddle bags
- ♥ Once on the lips, forever on the hips
- ♥ Don't dillydally at the Deli
- ♥ Pieces of pie stay on the thigh
- ♥ A bonbon is never gone
- ♥ Tempting aroma! What to do? Just breathe in and chew!

Along with the "No Smoking" sections, wouldn't it be a delight if restaurants had "No-Fat" sections? That way we wouldn't have to smell the fries or drool over desserts.

*Write your congressman!*

# Seven Top Clues that You are Over-Stressed

1. You get somewhere and notice you are wearing two different shoes.
2. You're putting on lip color and realize you are using black liner.
3. You can't find your sheets because you forgot a load of wash at the Laundromat.
4. You go to a party on the wrong date.
5. You discover you missed a meeting that was last week.
6. You realize that the irritating sound in the kitchen is the water boiling over.
7. You find the iron in the refrigerator.

When I came across the above list of ways to tell that you are overstressed, I realized that I have had them all happen to me at one time or another. I think it's just part of motherhood and life. I mean, hasn't every woman experienced these things? Please tell me yes!

# BUILDING A GLORIOUS YOU

The Ziegfield Follies were famous theatrical productions on Broadway back in the years from 1907-1931. Florenz Ziegfield used a secret to having his newly hired dancers perform their very best their first night. He would have a beautiful gift box of exquisite French lingerie delivered to their dressing room.

Mr. Ziegfield knew the power of building self-esteem and overcoming the feelings of intimidation. This really hits home with me as I know that when I was performing, I really loved the large earrings. (Back then, large earrings were nowhere to be found in the stores). I discovered that when I was wearing my imported large Middle-Eastern dangling earrings, I felt like I had the power to do anything. I knew no fear. Now, I know that most men would laugh at that. But I think that most women know exactly what I mean.

The topic of psyches, self-esteem and ego is a vast arena. All I know is that sometimes the smallest things can have the power to carry one to great heights. Define what lifts you up and use it.

*No one can intimidate you without your permission.*
—Eleanor Roosevelt

# THE GLOW FROM WITHIN

I am convinced there's a little belly dancer in every woman. Well, at least there was inside this one!

My husband doesn't like to dance, I love to dance and in Middle Eastern dance, you do not need a partner. It was perfect! I loved the dancing, the music, the performing and the costuming.

In American Belly Dance, there are many choices. Whether it's ethnic or cabaret style, whether it's Turkish, Bedouin, Gwahzee, or Egyptian. The cultures dictate the rhythms, dance steps and costuming. It seems like before I was halfway through designing and creating one costume, I was already planning the next one.

Initially, I made most of my costumes. The detailing, the sequins, and the hours of beading consumed all my spare time. Eventually I began buying at least the main pieces. Then the time came when I was able to purchase the authentic sets. Different coin belts advanced to a mirrored belt set, then a custom-made one with aurora borealis inset stones, and then there was the Turkish combo with heavy beads and coins. The dazzle was endless. When dancing with my partner as the Maharajah

Dancers, we worked with an importer who would select costumes to our specifications when she was on her buying trips. Each costume has its own personality and today holds its own memories.

Like many people, in the summer, we often see a glow in the sky above our home. It is the glow from a beautiful summer sun set. A friend always teased me that the glow above our house wasn't from the sun. It was from all of the sparkle in my closets.

*The sparkle of each costume also ignited*
*a glow within me. It was a good thing.*
*What ignites the glow within you?*

# SINGING YOUR SONG

It was somewhere between a chiropractor appointment and my work as a sales manager that I realized I probably wouldn't be able to dance forever. Even though I was approaching midlife, I was still pondering what was it that I wanted to do when I grew up. Through my dance programs, I had learned that I really enjoyed talking with audiences, entertaining, and getting to know people. Oh, how I wished I had a spectacular singing voice, but not all dreams are meant to come true. (Actually, I think my voice is more reminiscent of a nightmare.)

Then I heard a speaker, Rosita Perez, a well-known, national speaker, address a women's wellness audience. She gave a great message and sang a few songs. Then she spoke about the fact that we all have a song to sing.

As I sat there listening to her, it occurred to me that even though I didn't have an extraordinary singing voice, I could still talk. Maybe I could combine my work experience with my entertainment experience and help people deal with workplace issues and life, and help them put a little zip into their day. And, I thought, there may be a woman's group who might be interested in an old belly dancer who had things to say.

I called Rosita up the next day and asked her what I had to do to become a speaker. She became one of my mentors. I am ever indebted to her. Thank you, Rosita!

*Each of us has a song. Don't let your song go unsung.*

# THE MEETING PLACE

Have you ever made a quick dash to the grocery store to grab some items, only to return home an hour or more later? In trying to explain exactly what took so long to pick up just a few things, you try to recap the journey. For me, it often seems to go something like this:

Somewhere between the peas and broccoli, you run into an old friend who is visiting in town, a quick catch-up and the heart leaps with joy at the chance meeting. Then at the deli, you hear of a good recipe idea—perfect for your next gathering, let me write this down, would I need 1 or 2 onions? And, what do you know, somewhere between the toweling and bathroom cleaner, you learn that a mutual acquaintance passed away last night. There's the shock, an exchange of information, and a few tears with a hug. Between the pickles and noodles, you meet your neighbor and her brand new baby. He is so cute and so big already. In the frozen foods, you say a quick hello to the new member at card club. Then, just as you make your way into the checkout counter, who's ahead of you? None other than your next-door neighbor, whom you haven't seen in days.

*And jam wasn't even on my shopping list!*

# It's Just a Little Thing, or Is it?

Several years ago I heard about a woman in Michigan who had put an ad in the paper to advertise her listening service. All people had to do was call her and she would listen to them. She charged by the minute and it made the news because of how successful her business was already in the first few months.

Whether people just need to talk to someone or they are lonely, a listening ear can heal a heart. Sometimes it's the little things we can do that can make a big difference for someone else. I am reminded of this story:

A young volunteer was to call an elderly lady every morning, just to make sure she was all right. One day, the volunteer got busy and soon it was noon. The elderly lady called her and questioned why she hadn't called. The volunteer explained she was just about to make the call. The elderly lady said, "Oh good, I'll hang up so you can call. Your call is the only time my phone ever rings."

*If speaking is silver, then listening is gold.*
—Turkish Proverb

# THE PASSPORT

Has there ever been a sorrier likeness of anyone than the one on a passport? It is amazing how awful a passport picture can turn out. I think they have rigged cameras designed to demoralize, humble and depress. It's as though they already think you should look like you would when you are dead. Well, I'm not dead yet. While I never thought of myself as being vain, after seeing my first attempt at a passport photo, there was no way I was going to put that picture on anything.

A few weeks later, I went to another place and had a second attempt at a passport picture. This time I wore a higher collar, so the aging skin around my neck didn't prevail. The young man taking the picture was very tall. He was holding the camera higher than my eye level so I made sure to raise my chin up. Okay, so this one didn't turn out so hot either. If what they wanted was a likeness of what I looked like, that surely wasn't it. (So, who was that person in the picture?) I was convinced they must use military-issue cameras with built-in capacities for photo sabotage.

The months went by. Pretty soon, it was a year later. My husband reminded me that we really did need to get our passports. (Of course, he had gone in, took his, and was done.) The third try for me came on the morning that we stopped by the post office to drop off my husband's application. He suggested that as long as we were in town, we could stop by Walgreens to have my passport photo taken. Of course, he was unaware this was my third attempt and I wasn't going to be the one to tell him. Although I hadn't prepared for it, we were just on a routine errand run -- and forgetting for one brief senior moment the past debacles, I thought, "What the heck, just get a picture. How bad can it be?"

It can be bad.

The memories of my former attempts came flooding back. This time, it was a short, little gal holding the camera. She was much shorter than I, so I knew this meant trouble. Then she told me not to smile. I told her "Not smile? But that's me, it's what I do." So I obliged. When she finished, she handed me the blue folder with the picture. There it was. She had gotten a picture of what seemed to be someone with a flat head, stuffed cheeks, no eyes or eyebrows, all resting on an enormous double chin. There was no way that I was that person in that photo!!!!

Home I go. I'll show them. By now, I had figured out that I needed to pull out all stops and use the heavy-duty arsenal for this government project. I put on a great hot pink blouse – after all, at least then the blouse would be attractive in the picture. I redid my hair with more flair and hair sprayed it to the max, one hair didn't dare move. Then I grabbed my make-up tool kit and redid everything I had done a few hours earlier – layering it heavier than I would ever normally wear it. I would show them. From the eyelashes to the blush, from the eyebrows to the lipstick, everything went on a shade or two darker than usual. I was finally ready. I went back to Walgreens.

When I walked up to the clerk, she asked me why I was re-doing the picture. I told her it was awful and needed to be redone. She indignantly and emphatically stated that a new one wouldn't be any better. I assured her it would and insisted we try again. She pulled down the screen. This time, just as she was ready to snap, I popped a gentle smile, and quickly flexed my knees, bringing my head level with the camera (There will be no double chin on this one—well, hardly one, anyway). I attached that photo to my passport application and it was done.

Amen.

*Lordy, Lordy, it's not easy being over forty.*

# Isn't it the Truth?

*A collection of cyberspace wisdom*

♥ Just when you make ends meet, they move the ends.

♥ A woman has the last word in any argument; anything after that is the beginning of a new argument.

♥ It's better to be silent and appear stupid, than to open your mouth and prove it.

♥ I try to take it one day at a time, but sometimes several days attack me at once.

♥ Golf. It would be nice to play my normal game. Just once.

♥ If money talks, chocolate sings.

♥ Wouldn't it be nice if Sears finally made a vacuum you can just ride on?

♥ Housework is something you do that nobody notices until you don't do it.

- Brain cells come and brain cells go, but fat cells live forever.

- How much Healthy Choice ice cream can I eat before it's no longer a healthy choice?

- I used to have a handle on life, but it broke.

- Be careful of your thoughts; they may become words at any moment.

# It's Not Easy Being a Woman

This humorous look at womanhood set to a happy tune is sometimes shared with women audiences. It's been said: "Blessed are they who can laugh at themselves, for they shall never cease to be amused." Isn't that the truth?

*It's not easy being a woman, that we know is true.*
*We try to look perfect, and beautifully smile, too*
*and underneath it all, the panty hose is killing you.*

*It's not easy being a woman; being fat will never do*
*No matter how hard we try, we just can't win;*
*Give me an air brush and make me perfect 10.*

*It's not easy being a woman, we try to do it all*
*But when things go wrong and there's a glitsch,*
*so we're a little cranky, first thing they do*
*is call us a !!!!!!!.*

*It's not easy being a woman, but we love it just the same,*
*We do the best with what we've got; heart & soul is tops*
*But keep the windows open! We are getting mighty HOT!*

---

# The Pea on the Mountain

Every time my daughter Darla came home from college, sooner or later, we'd be getting ready to go somewhere and the traditional "How do I look?" would be exchanged. She would look at me, smile, and come up and pat my hair down so it wouldn't be so puffy. I would exclaim that I didn't want to look like I had a "pea on a mountain."

Darla would laugh and ask, "Where did you ever get that term from?"

My hair is very fine and flat. Every time I went to the hair salon, when it came time to style my hair, I would remind them to tease it well, use spray and do not make my head look like the "pea on the mountain." They would laugh, give a condescending nod to this eccentric old person and proceed to do their best.

One day, I was looking through my old high school pictures. There I was. I had the foxiest beehive hairdo you ever did see on top of my small frame. It was definitely a case of the "mountain on top of the pea."

*There's a little of who we used to be in each one of us.*
*May the years be forgiving and our youth patient with*
*care. It won't be long before they're sitting our chair.*

*We are today some of who we were yesterday*
*Just be careful in debating your desires with people who*
*don't have a clue.*
*Passersby may not be able to tell who is who.*

# Things I've Learned About Aging

♥ Just when we get our heads together, our bodies fall apart.

♥ Kids: You either deny birthing them or you have to start lying about their age, too.

♥ My slender, long arms vanished and no one is searching for them.

♥ I only heard about double chins; no one told me about the quadruple sets.

♥ The only thing worse in the summer than cellulite, is cellulite without a tan.

♥ Joining *Curves*® is not enough; you have to go.

♥ A bad hair style at the salon is temporary and not cause for a hissy fit. It, too, shall pass.

- ♥ People need to retire from jobs so they have time for all of their doctors' appointments.

- ♥ No one wants to hear "I told you so."

- ♥ Asking a hubby to help you diet is a mistake; you become really good at growling.

- ♥ Is your cellulite bothering you? Slap a sequin on it.

- ♥ Police show frazzled grandmas with their grandbabies no mercy for speeding.

- ♥ A memory is an easy thing to lose.

- ♥ Maybe our bodies need to expand to hold all of the wisdom and love we've acquired.

- ♥ Perhaps the reason time goes so fast the older one gets is to somehow prepare us for the phenomenal passage into eternal life.

# Shameful Vanity

A long with more candles on my cake, came the need for eye glasses.

First, it was the need for reading glasses. I found I needed a No. 3.00 hardware store special. All right, no problem. That was easy.

Then I went to get my driver's license renewed. I put my head into the machine, looked at the different things that appeared and answered the man's questions. Then he asked me what one sign said. I responded: "What sign?" Okay, so now I need glasses to see long distances to drive. Being a grab-and-go kind of gal, I knew I wasn't ready to molly-coddle a precious pair of expensive bifocals. I quickly discovered a No. 1.00 reading glass would work for my long-distance purposes just fine.

In driving along wearing my No.1.00 glasses, I realized that in order to see my watch, or where to turn on the car's window defroster (why do they put those buttons way down there, anyway?), I needed my No.3.00 glasses. It didn't take long for me to master the art of double-decking.

One day I went to the grocery store. I thought I must be looking all right as I noticed I was getting a few glances and even second takes from other shoppers—most quite a bit younger than I. I could almost feel the extra bounce beginning in each step.

Then I realized I was still wearing two pairs of eye glasses perched on my nose.

*There is nothing so agonizing to the fine skin of vanity as the application of a rough truth.*
*—E.G. Bulwer-Lyttonk*

*I didn't see any 'Vanity' bread on the shelf that day, but I would swear I smelled toast burning.*

# Ode to Womanhood

To all the young moms of today:

*Enjoy the wonderful years when your family is young,*
*Savor each moment, each laugh,*
*each tear and song that is sung.*
*Your devotion and love will forever*
*have its impact and hold so true*
*As your children grow to adulthood*
*and return their love to you.*

For the baby boomers and veteran ladies:

*The dog has died, the kids are grown and gone;*
*Dad doesn't care where Mom goes,*
*as so he doesn't have to go along.*
*So world look out—move over Dr. Seuss*
*From cyberspace to boutiques, Mom's on the loose!*

*Truer words were never spoken!*

---

D. Kinza Christenson 131

# Beauty Tips from Audrey

Audrey Hepburn wrote the following words when she was asked to share her "beauty tips." They were read at her funeral years later.

- ♥ For attractive lips, speak words of kindness.

- ♥ For lovely eyes, seek out the good in people.

- ♥ For a slim figure, share your food with the hungry.

- ♥ For beautiful hair, let a child run his/her fingers through it once a day.

- ♥ For poise, walk with the knowledge that you never walk alone.

- ♥ People, even more than things, have to be restored, renewed, revived, reclaimed and redeemed; never throw out anyone.

♥ Remember, if you ever need a helping hand, you will find one at the end of each of your arms.

♥ As you grow older, you will discover that you have two hands, one for helping yourself, and the other for helping others.

*Thank you, Audrey, for your profound wisdom.*

# HEARTSTRINGS

# A Very Special Olympic Lesson

Some people believe we are human beings placed on this earth to have the opportunity to experience what it's like to be spiritual, if they choose to do so. I believe we are spiritual brings given the opportunity to experience what it's like to be human.

It was the 1996 Seattle Special Olympics. Nine physically and mentally handicapped kids lined up to run the 100-yard dash. The gun fired. They took off running. The stands were filled with beaming parents and family members cheering as loudly as they could. The kids were each running as fast and hard as they could. One foot after the other, they ran with all their heart, mind and soul. Then one tripped, stumbled and fell, crying out as he went down. The other eight runners heard his cry and stopped. They turned around, went to him. A little girl with Downe's syndrome learned over, kissed him on the forehead and said, "This will make it all better."

Then, in front of a grandstand full of stunned onlookers, the eight kids helped their little friend up. They linked arms and walked the rest of the race, crossing the finish line together.

These young kids instinctively knew what some humans never learn.

*Love, compassion, and caring:*
*those sound like great ingredients*
*for a good batch of jam.*

# Our "Gifts from the Heart" Christmas

About ten years ago, I realized that I was no longer looking forward to our family get-together for gift openings. We were at a time in our family where our own children were all grown and in college. We had no small children to provide the entertainment and squeals. Even though we drew names for a gift exchange, it seemed the presents were getting more expensive and not personal. We'd open them, say thank you and then return them the next day!

Just before Christmas one year, I sent out an invitation to everyone stating this was going to be a "Gifts from the Heart" Christmas.

The rules were:

- ♥ You could only spend $10.
- ♥ The gift had to be hand-made or at least personalized.
- ♥ Each was responsible for his or her own giving gift (wife, mom, sister cannot do it for you).

- ♥ No switching names.
- ♥ Your gift must be accompanied with a tribute of some kind—a song, poem, or activity.

I can remember thinking that no one would probably show up that day. But much to my surprise, they did and they transformed our quiet day into a day of laughter and joy!

Interestingly, the guys who had complained the loudest came through with tributes that truly touched the heart—some funny, some sincere. None were poets by trade, but all kept in the spirit of the day. I remember nephew Jim had a special treat for us. For his tribute, he decided to do a headstand. And he did. His creative thinking was a hit. It brought laughter and cheers from everyone.

The kids are all grown now. Daughter-in-law Jennifer and son-in-law Aaron have joined our family, and being great sports, have graciously jumped on our Christmas tradition bandwagon. We have a new generation of little ones in our midst. The guys take turns playing Santa Claus each year and when it gets close to Santa making his appearance, we all break into a chorus of "Jingle Bells." The grandkids squeal with delight. The tributes have risen to a new level with poems, the occasional skit, or even a rapper performance.

We have put laughter back into our Christmas! We have discovered it is no longer the gifts that are the highlight of the day, it is the "tributes" and we have started a family album to keep these cherished mementos.

The true gift of all of this has been to watch everyone blossom over the years as they grew in their abilities and confidence to express warmth, laugh at themselves, and create bonds other family members.

Don't be afraid to take a risk to make something better. The others will probably thank you for it, or not. It really doesn't matter as long as you've tried. Just do it.

*We have only so much time together,*
*so make the most of every moment.*
*If something could be better, make it better!*


*(This invitation is a free download available at my website: www.kinza.net/freestuff.html)*

# HUGS

As a small girl, I remember visiting my friends and seeing them hug their moms and dads. This looked very strange to me because my family was very conservative. Our folks were gentle and loving but never showed outward affection, typical, I believe, of many in that generation during those years.

One day, when I was grown, I was talking with my sister, Marilyn. We both had small children then and shared a desire for that type of closeness in our family. We decided it was time to change things. From that day on, when we went out to the farm to visit our folks, we would greet them with a big hug.

I remember the first time I said "Hi Dad" and went up and gave him a big hug. He looked surprised and pleased, and perhaps a bit puzzled. What was I going to ask for now? Then I went over to Mom and gave her a big hug. You should have seen her smile. Of course, the kids saw this display of affection and followed suit. Marilyn and her family did the same. Soon, it spread to all of our family gatherings, an expected gesture of affection.

Our children are grown now but they do not know the world without hugs.

*I thank God for the courage to help*
*initiate hugs in our family.*
*Is there something you would like to*
*promote with your loved ones?*

# THE TREE-TRIMMING TRADITION

Starting traditions creates memories that will last a lifetime. There is one tradition I thought was especially nice that we started when my children were toddlers. It was our tree-trimming party and it would be complete with eggnog and pfeffernuesse cookies.

The kids would be so excited as we hauled the freshly cut tree into the house. It smelled so good. The ornament boxes were brought up from the basement. We would turn on the Christmas carols and the tree trimming would begin. The routine was always the same: First the lights— oh, how they'd sparkle; then the ornaments—each child had favorites. This was followed by the precise (or not) draping of some beads; and topped off with delicately hung tinsel.

Our hearts seemed to dance to the merriment of the Christmas carols. The kids' eyes twinkled with excitement and anticipation. It was a heartwarming, cozy evening. When finished, we would sit sipping the eggnog and snack on pfefferneusse cookies as we admired the beauty of the radiant Christmas tree.

Years later, when my daughter, Darla, was home from college, she offered to help me trim the tree. I was so grateful. I wasn't looking forward to trimming it myself. The tree trimming was delightful, listening once again to the Christmas carols, being together and sharing the latest news of friends and what was happening in our lives. As every year before, I brought out the eggnog and the pfeffernuesse cookies.

Amidst the laughter, Darla suddenly got very serious and said she had something to tell me. I sat down on the couch to prepare myself for whatever this college student was about to say.

It was then that she made a confession to me. Very gently and caringly, she looked me in the eye and said, "Mom, I've never liked pfeffernuesse cookies."

All those years, rather than hurt my feelings and spoil my tradition, she had endured the cookies in silence. What a gift of love! (We have started using a different kind of cookie since then.)

*The best gifts aren't always*
*found under the Christmas tree.*

# TAH-DAH

My mom was still living in her beautiful farm home when she discovered she had ALS (Lou Gehrig's disease). My dad had passed away a few years before and, as her children living nearby, we became her caregivers. It was the worst of times and, in an unexpected, emotionally, indescribable way, the best of times. We had never been closer. It was about nurturing, supporting, enduring and love. Through it all, she kept her sense of humor and continued to be the lovely, dignified person we had always known.

It was autumn and we kept a bowl of apples on the porch for visitors; and did all the little day-to-day things that were needed to get Mom through this time. When Mom reached the point where she was getting too weak to climb the stairs at night, we offered to bring her bed down and make a bedroom downstairs for her. She wouldn't hear of it. She wasn't ready for that yet. That would mean she was giving up.

With her muscles so weak she could hardly grasp a spoon, her walk a deliberate slow shuffle, evening would come and she would go to the foot of the stairs. Grasping onto the rail with one hand, she would then reach over to grab hold of the rail with her other hand also, the best she could. Mom would then slowly pull herself up to the next step. It was a series of very strained and focused "reach and pulls." We stood beside her but let her do it herself. Every night, it took her longer and required more effort.

When we got to the top of the stairs, she would let out a big sigh. Then we'd look at each other and I would see that wonderful twinkle in her eyes, and together we would cheer: "Hurray, Yes! We did it!" and we would laugh in a little celebration of our own. We both knew Mom was going to lose the war, but we had learned how important was to celebrate all of the victories along the way.

*Life is too short. Celebrate everything.*
*How many "Tah-Dah" moments have you had today?*

# Sweet Corn and Life

Over the 4th of July holiday, while my daughter and I were selecting sweet corn from our local store, Darla pointed out to me that many of them were not good at the end of the ear. She was tempted to put some of them back saying, "They should be perfect all the way to the end." We concluded that most of the ears looked good and that, if we had to, we could easily cut out the bad parts.

I couldn't help but think how profound her statement was. "It should be perfect all the way to the end." That pretty much describes how we all hope our lives are, perfect all the way to the end. Unfortunately, in life, things do not always go as we planned. Sometimes our plans are taken away. How nice it would be if we could just "cut out' the bad parts." Instead, we must find the strength to endure them. As with the kernels of corn, we need to find the glory in the sweet and succulent parts of life that remain.

*Please pass the jam.*

# Little Princess

When I was a child of about five or six, we were once again attending our family reunion. This was a big annual trip for us. It was at a time that life was spent on the farm, in church or in school. There wasn't a television or a store to go to for entertainment. Life was simple.

The reunion was a three-hour car drive on a hot August Sunday summer day. I always looked forward to this because we didn't get the chance to go anywhere very often and this day we would see all of our cousins. There would be games, chatter and fun.

This particular day, my Uncle Smokey was scooping up ice cream cones for anyone who wanted one. It was hot and the vanilla ice cream looked so good. I asked if I could have one. Uncle Smokey swooped me up and sat me on the counter; exclaiming: "Little Princess, you can have anything you want" and proceeded to prepare a wonderful-looking, vanilla ice cream cone.

Now, no one had every called me a "princess" before. And, "I could have anything I wanted?" Wow, that really hit me. I never forgot his words. Perhaps it was because of my conservative upbringing but for some reason, with a childlike trust, I believed him.

A few years ago, we attended the wedding anniversary of Smokey and his wife, Bernice. I took this opportunity to tell Smokey about how his words that day stuck with me entire life. He had not remembered the instance, but I could tell his heart was warmed to think that I had recalled it. I suppose it is likely that he said that to all of the little children who wanted ice cream that day. But I thanked him for the impact those words had on my life.

Smokey passed away this year. His words still remain in my heart.

*Once you are gone, all that remains*
*is that which you have given away.*
*I was so glad I had the opportunity to say "thank you."*
*Is there someone you need to thank today?*

# A MEANINGFUL CONVERSATION

When you think of it, most of our "talk" is pretty light. We exchange practical information and we chatter about general "stuff," who's going to win the ballgame, the latest hair style; the work that we do and the goings on of everyday living.

A colleague shared a story of a challenge their MasterMind group tossed out to its members. Before their next get together, they had to have a meaningful conversation with a complete stranger. Wow, now there's an assignment! My Jewish colleague's incredible story unfolded.

He was dining in a little quaint Chicago restaurant. As he looked around, he decided this might be a good time to try to fulfill his assignment. There was a rather large group of people dining not far from him. He picked out his 'stranger,' an older man. He went up to the table and introduced himself to the man and explained his mission and asked if they could talk. He was offered a chair. They talked about various things for awhile. Then the man got very serious and said he had lived in turmoil and guilt for many years. There was always something he wanted to do but had never done it and asked if he could do it now. He said "I want to apologize to you." My friend knew he had never met the man before so he asked: Apologize for what?"

Then the man told his story: "When I was eight years old and living in Germany, the Nazi's pounded on our door and demanded to know if there were any Jews in our building. Not knowing what it meant, I nodded and pointed upstairs to where my little friend and his family lived." After that there was a commotion and we saw the soldiers take them away. We never saw them again. My whole life I have lived with guilt for what I did." With tears now welling up in his eyes, he continued: 'To you I must now say, I am so sorry for what I did to those people...to your people...I didn't know."

There, in that little restaurant, two souls connected.

*Have you had meaningful conversation*
*with someone today?*

# To Go Back for Just One Day

The clear blue summer skies and majestic white fluffy clouds reign above the farmstead where the sweet smells of mowed grass and fresh cut hay fill the nostrils. Dad's working in the fields on the new tractor. We took lemonade out to him in the heat of the day. Tonight after milking is done, he will help me practice with my calf to show at the county fair. Meanwhile, I'll ride my horse— what a sense of freedom, galloping across the freshly cut fields with the wind blowing through my hair! Mom's cooking the asparagus she picked along the fence line today, the aroma of supper fills the kitchen. Petite in her flowered cotton dress, cooking at the stove, never judging, always listening, we know for us she's always there.

*Oh, to be able to go back for just one summer day.*

The crispness of fall is in the air, golden leaves crunch under the feet and the big maple is in its shroud of brilliant color. The big corn picking machines are in the fields. The roar of the tractor fills the air as it pulls another load of corn to the silos almost in an urgency to beat the soon approaching cold. A busload of visitors from foreign countries are coming to tour our farm today. Dad has cleaned the stalls and made the milk house shine. Mom is weeding flowers and painting the porch steps. Her little barn cat friends are meowing at her feet, just begging for one more treat.

*Oh, to be able to go back for just one fall day.*

The snowflakes dance down from the sky and cover the farm like a cozy fresh, sparkling white blanket. The corn is in the silos, the winter supply of hay is stored in the barn. It's dark when Dad gets up to milk the cows and shovels his path to the barn. The Holstein cows all in their stanchions stand, the milking machines throb and the sound of the radio and mooing fill the air. Fresh milk flows through the pipelines. The milk truck will soon be here. Dad will bring a bucket of fresh milk in for drinking. Mom will have a nice hot breakfast waiting for him and there will be a discussion of world events, politics, and family. The milk tester comes tonight.

*Oh, to be able to go back for just one winter day.*

The earth is bursting forth in glory as it heralds the arrival of spring. The cows are frolicking in the pasture, the apple blossoms are in bloom, birds are nesting everywhere, planting season is here. There are long days of tilling and planting, my Dad working on the machinery to keep it running. Mom walks to the mailbox to mail her letters and spread her love to others. She adds a new joke to her refrigerator to make us laugh. A bouquet of violets in that lovely, delicate little blue glass vase adorns her kitchen table, with today's newspapers piled nearby. Mom does her ironing then she gets ready to drive to town for groceries. A new calf was born today.

*Oh, to be able to go back for just one spring day.*


*Thank you, God, for a memory.*
*It allows me to back and visit at will.*
*But tell me how to keep the visions from fading,*
*When I long to experience it still.*

# THE GLORY OF HIS LOVE

A patient dies on the operating table, but surgeon John Riesch is able to revive him. When the patient regains consciousness, the doctor asks whether he remembers anything.

"I had the nicest visit with Tommy," the patient replies.

"Tommy. Who's that?" the doctor inquires.

"You don't know him. We lost our son so many years ago. He said, 'Dad, I've been waiting for you for so long. It's nice to see you.' "

*Bring on the jam.*

Excerpt from the book "White Coat Wisdom" by Steve Busalacchi.

# TALLY OF THE ANGELS

I was nine months pregnant. Feeling fine and sparky, we went to our friends' New Year's Eve party. It was a grand party but I soon found myself going into labor so we headed for the hospital. It looked like now we might just also be having the town's New Year's baby!

Being in labor has a way of consuming all one's attention. I guess I should have noticed that eventually the nurses stopped coming in to check the baby's heartbeat, but I didn't. Our baby, Donna Jean, was stillborn.

When you hear news like that, you become wretched with pain, agony and disbelief. During this time, two nurses were gently continuously stroking my arms. I always remember the calming impact those nurses had. They were definitely my angels that traumatic night. If there's a Tally of Angels for my life, they'll be on it.

I think there are times when we all need earthly angels, and there are times when we all can be the earthly angel who comes to the aid of others. When the grand Tally of Angels is taken, may we all have our names there.

*An angel is someone who helps you up when your wings have forgotten how to fly.*

---

D. Kinza Christenson 157

# THE ROSE

There was always a lovely pink tea rose bush right by the door to what we called our bathhouse at our little home on the lake. The bush was always full of blooms, each one more fragrant and beautiful than the next.

As the landscaping evolved, we decided to transplant the rose bush to another location. I think it died after the first winter.

Spring came and lo and behold, from a crack in the concrete floor of the bath house, just inside the door frame, sprung a rose branch upon which soon bloomed a brilliant pink rose. We let it grow there. It just seemed right to let it continue its resurrection. At one point, we actually notched a pathway in the screen door so we could guide the branch outside where there would be more sun.

Through the years, it has grown into more of a little bush. Near the bath house, there is just enough sun to bring more roses. Somehow, this rose bush and its roses symbolize life to me. Every spring, when we once again see the rose stems emerge, I am reminded of the following poem.

# THE ROSE BEYOND THE WALL

## By A.L. Frank

Near shady wall a rose once grew,
Budded and blossomed in God's free light,
Watered and fed by morning dew,
Shedding its sweetness day and night.

As it grew and blossomed fair and tall,
Slowly rising to loftier height,
It came to a crevice in the wall
Through which there shone a beam of light.

Onward it crept with added strength
With never a thought of fear or pride,
It followed the light through the crevice's length
And unfolded itself on the other side.

The light, the dew, the broadening view
Were found the same as they were before,
And it lost itself in beauties new,
Breathing its fragrance more and more.

Shall claim of death cause us to grieve
And make our courage faint and fall?
Nay! Let us faith and hope receive—
The rose still grows beyond the wall,

Scattering fragrance far and wide
Just as it did in days of yore,
Just as it did on the other side,
Just as it will forevermore.

# SPREADING THE JAM

# THE MAGIC OF A SMILE

A smile costs nothing, but gives much.
It enriches those who receive,
without making poorer those who give.
It takes but a moment, but the memory of it
sometimes lasts forever.
None is so rich or mighty that he gets along with it
and none is so poor, but he can be made rich by it.
A smile creates happiness in the home, fosters good
will in business and is the countersign of friendship.
It brings rest to the weary, cheer to the discouraged,
sunshine to the sad,
and is nature's best antidote for trouble.
Yet it cannot be bought, begged, borrowed or stolen,
for it is something that is no value to anyone
until it is given away.
Some people are too tired to give you a smile;
give them one of yours, as no one needs a smile so much
as he who has no more to give.

*A smile is the shortest distance between two people.*
—Victor Borge

# WILLARD C. MCLAINE

My sisters, Marilyn and Allene, and I were in Alexandria, Virginia. Being so close to Washington, D.C., we decided to take the Metro Transit System into the city and see some sights. Once at the Eisenhower Street Metro Station, we discovered we had to use vending machines to receive our passes for the ride. Not being familiar with these machines, we had not a clue what to do. There were slots and buttons everywhere with no decipherable, step 1-2-3 directions. We made several futile attempts to get our tickets and found ourselves getting more and more frustrated. Then, after inserting a $20 bill and getting nothing, we decided it was time to plead for help from the man in the booth.

Lethargic, indifferent, rude? No way. Instead, this man jumped up enthusiastically, bounded out of the booth and led us back over to the machines…laughing and joking all the way. He not only retrieved our change and the passes, he taught us how to do it, and led us through the process like a patient teacher would lead a young child, slowly and deliberately so we would remember for the next time.

When we were finally riding up the escalator to get on the Metro, we heard him call out. As we turned to look, we could see him waving at us, "I'll be waiting here for you when you return!" His words rang out like a cloak of warmth and welcome to strangers on a cold night.

Mr. Willard C. McClain knew the secret to providing extraordinary customer service—if you are ever in the Eisenhower Avenue Metro Station in Alexandria, VA, please give my regards to Willard!

*Like the taste of a succulent, sweet jam,*
*when you exceed the expectations of others,*
*you will be remembered.*

# CHUCKLE BAGS

It was Christmas and my brother-in-law Ken was beginning to start chemo treatments. I had picked his name for our gift giving. I tried to think of something that would be appropriate for him and came up with what I now call a Chuckle Bag™. It was a gift bag which I filled with 60 individually folded jokes and one-liners.

As time went on, I learned how much he and my sister appreciated that little gift. When their life was filled with worry and a sense of helplessness, not knowing what the future would bring, this bag became their source for a little temporary diversion and put a smile on their faces.

Each morning, they would select a Chuckle for the day and pull it from the bag. Ken would often use it on the nurses at the Chemo Center or with others he would meet during treatments.

Samples from a Chuckle Bag™:

♥ Cooking lesson #1: Don't fry bacon in the nude.

♥ What steps do you take when a bear is chasing you?...Very big ones!

He would adapt these and use them to bring some normalcy to his day. As he recovered from his chemo treatments, he told me they were enjoying recycling the chuckles. It was like a gift that keeps on giving.

Since that Christmas, I have sent Chuckle Bags™ out to many different people (and even have them available at our website: www.kinza.com).

It really warms the heart when you can help someone's load to be a little lighter and their road a little brighter.

*Laughter—it does a body good.*

# GOING ABOVE AND BEYOND

Because she had missed a connecting flight from Houston to Beaumont, Texas, a passenger resigned herself to the fact that she would be missing the funeral she was trying to attend. A Delta airlines fight attendant came to her rescue and personally drove her to the funeral.

What do you think this passenger now tells others about Delta Airlines?

*The extra mile is a road seldom traveled.*
*Take a suitcase full of jam.*

# Random Acts of Kindness

If you are looking for a guaranteed way to lift your spirits today—think of doing some random acts of kindness. Think of it, paying for the next guy's newspaper or coffee; drive through the toll booth and pay for the car behind you—being kind can be kind of fun! It takes little or no effort. Showing kindness can be as simple as holding a door open for someone.

There's a story is told about a woman who went into a fast food restaurant and the two homeless men ahead of her. They were unkempt, and obviously without much money. They each ordered a coffee. When it was the lady's turn to order, she ordered for herself and asked for two meals on a separate tray. She took the tray over to the two men. The men, with grateful hearts, had tears in their eyes when they thanked her.

Have fun and act spontaneously! That's why it's called a "random act."

*Just do it!*

# THE SWEETEST SOUND

As I was standing in the grocery store line, I could hear the clerk calling the customer she was waiting on by name. She then asked her how her daughter was doing. I figured they were friends. Then I listened as she waited on the next customer, heard her call the customer by her first name. She then asked her if she had made that dessert yet. I am pretty much a regular and was admittedly pleased when she called me by name. She then asked if I was tired of shoveling snow yet.

I have observed the clerk in my visits since. She has mastered the magic of knowing—and remembering—her customers' names and then she takes that even a step further. She connects with each customer with a personalized question or comment.

Since most people shop at the same grocery stores week after week, it would seem this type of customer service would be standard operating procedure. I have often wondered why more grocery stores don't make more effort to promote such excellence in their clerks. It makes customers feel like they are appreciated and valued.

*The sweetest sound ever heard is the sound of one's own name. It's pure jam to the soul.*

# GIFTS

A friend of mine worked for a disaster relief agency at the time the 9/11 disaster happened. She was sent to New York to assist with the response and recovery efforts. One of her jobs was to summarize Mayor Rudy Giuliani's comments and share them with agencies that needed to know the most current information about the disaster.

When I asked her what was the one biggest lesson she learned while in New York during this time, she shared with me how she was so touched by all of the ways people pitched in to help. From the pictures sent from grade-school children to neighbors sweeping and shoveling soot, to the people serving the food – each helping in his or her own way. It reminded her of a saying that she had heard long ago that summarized her feelings.

Her biggest lesson learned: "Give what you can. It may be greater than you think."

*One little act, how simple it may be;*
*Can have a profound effect of enormity;*
*One little act, to ease pain or bridge a sorrow;*
*Can lift a heart and impact a tomorrow.*
—D. Kinza Christenson

# SPREADING THE JOY OF THE TAMBOURINE

**P**eople often ask me about the significance of my tambourine. The tambourine is referred to as the "tambrel" in the Bible and was used for celebrations in biblical times. It, therefore, was a prop I often used in Middle Eastern dance routines. Today, in many of my programs, I use it and people have often called me the "Tambourine Lady."

My tambourine is one of my signatures and part of who I am as a keynote speaker. My original tambourine has been with me through 25 years as a dancer and performer. While I collect tambourines, this particular one is the one I generally use. It was made, interestingly, in China, probably in the 1960s, fits my hand perfectly, and has beautiful sounding cymbals.

The round shape of the tambourine represents the circle of life. All the colorful ribbons adorning it represent all the achievements we make in life, all the good service we provide, and all the good we do. Since we all have ribbons on our circles of life, the challenges become:

- How do we keep up our enthusiasm and keep adding new ribbons to our circle?
- How do we keep the ribbons from fading?

This one object, adorned with brightly colored ribbons, becomes a perfect vehicle for meaningful, fun messages to keep one's life in balance, attain ones personal goals and personal happiness, and celebrate life to the fullest.

## The Tambourine

*May its shape represent the circle of your life;*
*Its ribbons represent all of your accomplishments;*
*The love you share and the good you do.*

*May you celebrate your life with joy and exaltation*
*And may the good come back ten-fold to you.*

—D. Kinza Christenson

# JEFFREY

My husband and I were on our annual Christmas outing to the mall. Being a non-shopper, this was always an enlightening day for my hubby and we made it a special event, topped off with dinner in the evening.

We were in the men's department at Macy's when we noticed a sale rack. They had some great shirts on sale but found none in his size. As we were leaving the department, the young clerk came running after us, waving two shirts, excitedly calling out, "I found some shirts in your size!"

Don tried them on. One was a really snazzy white one that fit him to a tee. As we bought the shirt, the amiable clerk admired it, saying a shirt like that was probably what he should have on under his sport coat rather than the knit shirt he was wearing.

Apparently in agreement, the woman clerk standing nearby commented that one in the clerk's size was still hanging on the rack.

We found out that the young clerk's name was Jeffrey. He had a big smile and the type of charisma that most people can only dream about. We chatted and joked with Jeffrey. He put our shirt in a bag and as he handed it to us, he looked us in the eye, and said, "Thank you, Mr. and Mrs. Christenson, I'll definitely remember you the next time you come here!" We thanked him and left.

As we were going down the aisle, I whispered to my husband, "Let's buy him that shirt." We flagged down the other clerk. Excited to help us, the clerk took the shirt and us to another department so we could pay for it and have it packaged without being seen. She was so excited, saying to us, "You have no idea what a good thing this is that you are doing. Just wait until I get there. I don't want to miss this."

They called Jeffrey over. He looked a little puzzled. Then, I walked up to Jeffrey, handed the package to him and said, "This one's for you, Jeffrey. Merry Christmas."

There was disbelief and then there were hugs.... and, at least in my eyes, a few tears.


*Our hearts felt good. That was Christmas.*


*What an amazing world this would be if we celebrated the joy of Christmas every day!*

# THE IMPACT OF OUR WORDS

We were invited to a birthday party. As my hubby and I we were about to leave for the party, I saw my supply of little blue stickers that I use in some of my programs. On them are the words "Has anyone told you today, 'You Are Terrific?" Knowing that we probably wouldn't know many of the people at the party, I grabbed a supply of these stickers, thinking they might come in handy.

I was right. We didn't know many of the other guests. So throughout the evening, I would take a sticker out and walk up to the guests one by one. Showing the sticker, I looked them in the eye and said the words "Has anyone told you today, "You Are Terrific?" and proceed to put the sticker on a lapel or shoulder.

I received the same reaction each time. First it was the puzzled look, (like "What is this crazy lady doing?") then the face eventually broke into a smile and I'd hear a genuine "Thank you" and the conversation began. It was a great icebreaker.

Toward the end of the evening, one of the women who had received a sticker came up to me and said: "I want to thank you for the sticker. You have no idea how I needed to hear those words tonight."

*We never know the impact of our words.*
*When is the last time you looked someone*
*in the eye and told them how much*
*he or she means to you?*

# DO WHAT IS GOOD

Do all the good you can;
By all the means you can;
In all the ways you can;
In all the places you can;
At all the times you can;
To all the people you can;
As long as ever, you can.

—John Wesley

*You multiply your happiness by sharing it with others.*

*A certain magic happens when you help others fly ...*
*Their wings lift you up!*

# GRATITUDE IS AN ATTITUDE

*When you stop comparing what is right here*
*and now with what you wish it were, you can*
*begin to enjoy what is.*
—Carol Huber

Why is it that living in the world's most affluent country, we so easily fall into the pattern of complain, complain, complain? If it's not the weather, it's the traffic, the poor service, or something. As we look at other countries, we realize that as a society, we have gotten so spoiled. We tend to expect everything and seemingly appreciate nothing. When we lose gratitude, we lose the depths of our joy. Happiness does not bring gratitude. Gratitude brings happiness.

Imagine how different your life would be if you expressed gratitude for every person you meet and every thing you do, see and feel?

One fall day, I was walking with friends on a path covered with fallen leaves. Rather than just walking over them, we noticed one friend, Dee, walking through the thickest piles, kicking them up as she went. She delighted in their crisp sound, smell, and very being. She was taking pleasure at her ability to frolic in leaves on a sunny new day. The beauty of each intricacy of this fall day was magnified for her. It was just months before that she had been in the midst of chemo treatments. As a result of her ordeal, the simplest things have become appreciated joys.

Being grateful has a lot to do with where one focuses one's attention. How can you can cultivate an attitude of gratitude?

- ♥ Be kind.
- ♥ Count your blessings.
- ♥ Spend time helping others.
- ♥ Use "please," "thank you" and "you're welcome"
- ♥ Be appreciative of everything and everyone.
- ♥ "Be" in the moment. Absorb the here and now.
- ♥ Focus on the good.
- ♥ Recognize your time on earth will be brief.

*Spread gratitude like jam, everywhere you can.*

# GIVING THE GIFT OF FORGIVENESS

We've all heard the saying "To err is human; to forgive divine." Now there is another version: "To err is human; to forgive is much smarter.

Forgiveness is a word we don't hear or practice nearly enough. Instead, we carry grudges or anger around, which adds stress we are far better off without.

Grudges tend to fester inside us—kind of like thorns in our sides. Grudges generate negativity and distort our perceptions. They make life unpleasant and they make us not very nice people to be around. (Did you know that people who carry grudges scowl more?) With as many as 85 percent of all hospitalizations due either directly or indirectly to stress, it's much healthier to be grudge-free.

What better gift can you give yourself than banishing grudges from your life forever? So what do we do with those little grudges that keep sticking in our craws? And how do we avoid becoming grudge-grouches in the future? Thanks for asking. Here are some tips:

- Set your ego aside and stop taking things so personally.
- Give the other person the benefit of the doubt. Put yourself in his or her shoes.
- Face grudges head on, right away.
- Take ownership for the part your actions might have played in creating the situation.
- Forgive and ask forgiveness. Forgive someone today. If you like the way it makes you feel, forgive someone tomorrow.

For those serious, heavy-duty grudges, make a list. Then, for those people on your list about whom you're still harboring a grudge, do the following:

- If the person is dead, write a sincere letter.
- If the person lives over 300 miles away, make a phone call.
- If the person lives within 300 miles, drive to meet with him or her.

Remember, the purpose of your contact is not to say "I resent you for ..." but rather to make amends for what you did to offend the other person.

*Whether you're the giver or receiver,*
*forgiveness is a good thing.*

# BEYOND ETIQUETTE

I remember years ago going into a small, local restaurant in our little town. We were greeted by a young gentleman named Jim. I thought surely Jim was a highly trained and educated *maître d'*, probably flown in from New York. He was so polished. He had natural finesse and grace when welcoming and serving the patrons. He outshone any that I had ever seen before—or since. It was obvious he loved his work.

We learned he wasn't from a big city at all. He was a local guy who just liked what he did. Jim was sincere and his style simply reflected who he was.

Jim had mastered the art of showing respect, and a little bit more. He had the unique gift of making each person feel like royalty. As a result, we returned to the restaurant often. We liked being treated like royalty—everybody does!

*Royalty and jam go together hand in hand.*

People might remember what you do,
They might remember what you say;
But they will never forget how you made them feel.
—Maya Angelou

# GROW YOUR FUNNY BONE

Having a healthy funny bone is something that anyone can develop with a little practice. Looking at life with a comic twist will help ease stress, create a healthier you, help you through the hard times and make it easier to connect with others. Humor can help bridge those difficult conversations and lift the spirits of others. It's absolutely the easiest way to "spread jam." Have fun as you start practicing these techniques:

- ♥ Compare two things. *Mad as a wet hen.*
- ♥ Define something. *Marriage is an institution*
- ♥ Exaggerate: *Even the "Jaws of Life" couldn't pry that cookie out of my hand.*
- ♥ Make a list of 5 funny ways to…. *exercise...go bald...get fired, etc.*
- ♥ Observe. *Every cemetery has "Dead End" signs*
- ♥ Imagine worse. *Good news, you're hired. Bad news, You're not our first choice.*
- ♥ Start collecting jokes and 1-liners, and don't be afraid to poke fun a little fun at yourself!

*Humor is a tool given to help us on our life journey.*

# Optimist Creed

Promise Yourself ...
To be so strong that nothing can disturb your mind.
To talk health, happiness and prosperity
to every person you meet.
To make all your friends feel that
there is something in them.
To look at the sunny side of things and
make your optimism come true.
To think only of the best, to work only for the best and
to expect only the best.
To be just as enthusiastic about the success of others
as you are about your own.
To forget the mistakes of the past and
press on to the greater achievements of the future.
To wear a cheerful countenance at all times and
give every living creature you meet a smile.
To give so much time to the improvement of yourself
that you have no time to criticize others.
To be too large for worry, too noble for anger,
too strong for fear and too happy to
permit the presence of trouble.

—Christian D. Larson

# Let Your Light Shine

In Sunday School, I remember singing the song, "This Little Light of Mine, I'm Going to let it Shine…." and loved the tune as a child. At the time, I didn't realize the enormity of its meaning.

My brother, Bill, has always enjoyed music and plays a variety of instruments. At our family gatherings, he sets up his keyboard and entertains us all as his fingers magically make marvelous melodies of all kinds. Although he says it is the result of many years of practice, he now seems to be able to sit down and play piano "by ear."

Then there's his harmonica. Whether delighting the children or sitting under the stars on a quiet night, his harmonica makes hearts dance. The music he provides is like frosting on a cake. It just makes a day better. Known about town as the "Music Man," Bill plays for anyone who wants to listen—lifting the hearts and spreading the jam.

One night, we had a birthday party and everyone was supposed to share a talent. Some read poems, one did a magic trick, one even performed a jig. Then it came to my dad. In his eighties at the time, we all wondered what he'd do. Although very talented in his younger years, that night, he smiled and then ... he twiddled his thumbs. We all broke out in gales of laughter. Dad always came through for us. What a great sport he was!

One of life's lessons is that when you have a gift or talent, don't hide it. If you wait for someone to ask to see it, it might never happen. Swallow your pride, believe in yourself and offer it up. Too often, we listen to those little voices in our heads that warn us we may not be good enough, and we become fearful of looking foolish.

A music teacher I knew once told her extremely nervous student: "Don't be so conceited as to think it's all about you." That advice was a turning point in the pupil's career.

Everyone has something he or she does well, something to contribute, something that makes the person special.

Unzip yourself and let your light shine! You will be amazed at the difference it makes in your life.

*Life is not a dress rehearsal.*
*Share your light. It will light the way for others.*

# DREAMS

# SIGNS

As a small child, I loved pretending, dressing-up and playing make believe. Every year, our local town would have a White Elephant sale—for our younger readers, it's now called a rummage sale. Much to my delight, my mom would give me 50 cents with which I could buy anything I wanted. In those days, that was a lot of money, or so I thought. The White Elephant sale day was always an exciting day and something I looked forward to all year long.

And every year, I would spend my precious money on the same thing—a very glitzy, old prom dress. It would always be the gaudiest one on the rack—covered with sequins, bows, and trim. Oh, my heart would start palpitating at the sight. Often, I found a hat that went with it splendidly. I could hardly wait to get home to put on my new purchase. My wardrobe was renewed. I would have a new, marvelously grand dress to play in—complete with matching hat.

Recently, we took all of our old family movie pictures and put them onto video tape. When we viewed them, we couldn't stop laughing. In most of the shots of the family picnics and other family events, there was one little girl dancing and twirling in front of the camera, wearing a hat and dressed in the glitziest and gaudiest, long, cut-off dress you ever did see.

Some things never change. When I'm on stage wearing an elaborate costume of sparkle and holding a microphone in my hand, for me, that's a good day!

Studies show the happiest adults today are those who are doing something that is someway connected with what they enjoyed doing as a child. What did you enjoy doing as a child? What were your signs? Are you connected with your signs today?

*God planted seeds. We call them dreams.*

# Dreams Do Come True

*O*ur family was a fairly musical family. My dad played clarinet in a legion band and as kids, we all learned how to play the piano. It was natural, then, when my children started grade school, that I insisted our kids were going to know how to play piano. My daughter took to the piano beautifully. She had fun with it and seemed to enjoy playing the songs.

My son, on the other hand, fought me every inch of the way. One of the first popular songs he had to learn was "Star Wars." I'll never forget the tears shed over that theme song. Finally, we made a pact. He had to continue his lessons until the recital and play in the recital. After that, he could decide whether or not he wanted to continue with the piano lessons. Over the next several months, he learned many songs. The recital came and he played "The Entertainer" to perfection.

That next week, however, he said he wasn't going to play anymore. I kept my end of the bargain and let him stop his lessons. All through high school, he never went by the piano again.

David is now married and living in Minneapolis. One evening the phone rang. It was my son, talking fast and in an excited voice. "Mom, do you still have any of those old piano books lying around?" I told him I thought we did and asked him why. He replied, "We bought a piano today."

*Yes! Dreams do come true.*

# FOUR LITTLE WORDS

It was my 25th class reunion, held at a lovely yacht club. The planning committee had been working on it for months. When it came to planning the program, someone asked if I would be willing to perform as part of the after-dinner program. At that time, I was teaching and performing Middle Eastern Dance, so it seemed a natural for me and I looked forward to it. I never turned down an opportunity to dance. We planned that when I was done, I would have some of the former high school "stars" come up and have fun learning how to belly dance.

The night arrived. It was time. I appeared in my bright red sequin costume, dancing to a Greek routine. My veil flowed through the air and drum music filled the air. It was great fun for me and seemed to be enjoyed by everyone there.

Afterwards, one of my former classmates came up to me and said: "I would give my right arm to be able to do what you just did." Now, she was a classmate I hadn't known very well while in school, but in thinking about what she said, I felt badly for her.

How sad it was that so often we go through life, never stepping out of our comfort zone to stretch our wings. It takes a belief in ourselves and an "I can do it!" attitude. Probably no four words have a more profound effect on the sum of one's life experiences as those four powerful little words, "I can do it!"

*What is it that you wish you could do?*
*Five years from now, will you be rejoicing because*
*you have done it, or will you still be just wishing?*

# Unleash Your Spirit

I believe we all have an "inner spirit." (I always like to think of mine as being tall and thin!) This is where our character is formed. It is where the seeds of our human uniqueness lie: the seeds of wisdom, the seeds of humor, the seeds of compassion, and the seeds of our faith.

As we go through life, we need to nurture those seeds so we can blossom as individuals. It is when we nurture those seeds that our spirit is unleashed and we can make a difference in the lives of all whom we touch.

*What do you have to do to unleash your spirit*
*and be all that you can be?*

# Words to Live By

"I can't, I won't, I couldn't"
Said a tiny little voice;
For years I listened and obeyed,
And didn't even ponder a choice.

"I can't, I won't, I couldn't"
Such harmless little words;
Yet, if I let them rule my destiny,
My greatness will never be.

So, I can't, I won't , I couldn't"
I'm going to bid you adieu:
"I can" and "I will" now rule my life,
I have goals to meet and dreams to pursue.

—D. Kinza Christenson

# Someday ...

It seems like we spend much of the first half of our life thinking about things we are going to do "someday." It's easy to set hopes and dreams aside in our "Someday Bank," thinking we will do them "someday." You know... Someday when I'm rich...Someday when I'm thin (I don't wait for that one anymore)...Someday when I have more time...

Turning 50, for some reason, really hit me hard. Normally, I enjoyed my birthdays but my 50th was brutal. I think any birthday that ends with "0" is a bit of a shocker, whether it's 20, or 30, or 80. It means you have reached a milestone in your life.

I remember driving down the road in my car, giving myself a real pity party. I actually had tears well up in my eyes as I thought, "How in heck did I get to my 50th birthday?" I wondered with amazement where the last twenty or thirty years had gone. It was almost as though someone had stolen those years from me. A flicker of anger wanted to emerge inside me, yet I knew there was no such thing as a time thief.

Twenty years of "somedays" had disappeared in a flash. Like in the blink of an eye, they were gone.

Suddenly, it was like lightning struck my car. I had a revelation. In a blink of an eye, I could be another twenty or thirty years into the future. Wow, that thought changed my perspective completely. I was only 50! I had a good number of "somedays" still available to use. I just had to get busy. My eyes dried, I sparked up and was feeling fine. The flames on the candles on my cake that night were nothing compared to the fire that had been lit inside me.

*Someday is not a day of the week. Is there something you have been putting off until "someday"?*

*Yesterday is gone, tomorrow never comes. All we have is today, that's why it's called the present. Act now.*

# A Dream of a Job

It was an international affair at the exclusive Hyatt Regency. I guess you could say it was a dream of a job. Booked as the Maharajah Dancers, my dance partner, Sheena, and I were the after-dinner entertainment. It was a very fancy affair and we wore our top-notch, imported costumes, complete with gorgeous beading and coins. As glamorous as that may sound, there's always the behind-the-scenes part that no one ever sees.

For us that night, it was two costumed belly dancers, finger cymbals in place on beautifully polished fingers, making their way to the backstage area through the kitchen, trying to tippy-toe through the spilled coleslaw and cold clam chowder puddles on the floor and trying not to slip and fall or break our necks. We managed to arrive at stage side just as the music began.

The show went great. The audience clapped with the music. People were so appreciative of our efforts. The audience participation filled the room with laughter and applause.

I remember afterwards, Sheena and I stood in the huge two-story atrium corridor just outside the massive doors to the ballroom. Two young children were coming up the escalator. They were exclaiming, "Look, look!" as they pointed toward the ballroom doors and excitedly trying to get their parents' attention. Naturally, not wanting to miss anything, we turned our heads quickly to look behind us to see what the big attraction was.

Then, feeling a little foolish, we realized it was us!

*Oh, for the memories!*

# The Thing About Dreams

Most of us have many "dream seeds" within us. A dream is just a desire to do something some time in the future. For some people, a dream may be a very clear goal, a distinct path of pursuit. For others, it's less definite and not one specific thing. Life's ambitions sometimes take unusual paths. When we stand at the crossroads of those paths, it might be just a simple momentary choice that turns us down the path that takes us to where we are today. Sometimes, we don't even realize that where we are, is exactly where we hoped to be. Other times, we look around and wonder where the heck we are.

Just when we think we have our dreams planned out to be a reality, life happens. Perhaps a loved one is taken away, illness hits, or something happens and we realize the dreams we once had have been now taken away.

Unknown to me, there was a lady in one of my audiences who had lost her daughter several years before. The pain she had felt was unbearable. That night, I gave my "Laugh and Live Your Dream" program. It went well.

The audience was wonderful and seemed to enjoy and embrace my message. When the program was over, this same lady came up to me, took my hands as she told me her story and said: "Thank you so much. Tonight has been a turning point for me. Now, I can go on with my life."

*What thou the hour that once shone so bright,*
*be now forever taken from my sight.*
*Yet we will grieve not,*
*rather find, strength in what remains behind.*
—Excerpt from *Splendor in the Grass*
by F. Andrew Leslie

*A load becomes lighter when it's shared with another.*
*Perhaps it's the same with pain.*

# Your Dreams Can Come True

Your dream can come true,
It's all up to you;

Define it, frame it,
'Til you have a vision so fair;
Then get busy because you don't
Have a minute to spare.

Set a course, make a plan,
Pursue it every way that you can.
Set a time frame, and just watch how life
Weaves the opportunities for you to claim.

Your dream can come true.
It's all up to you.

—D. Kinza Christenson

# THIS BOOK MIGHT END HERE, BUT THE MESSAGES DO NOT!

To order books and other products or to learn more about Kinza's program offerings, visit her website at: www.kinza.net. You can also sign up for Kinza's popular free, online newsletter "Keys for Success."

Are you looking for a speaker for your next meeting or event? Turn the page to see what they are saying about Kinza's dynamic and enjoyable programs.

For more information & availability:
(800) 575-6817 or (262) 567-6317
kinza@kinza.net

# WHAT OTHERS ARE SAYING ABOUT KINZA'S SEMINARS AND KEYNOTES

"Our State employees were thoroughly entertained and educated --They enjoyed your humor and were moved by your message—It was highlight of the whole conference. *GOVERNMENT MEETING PLANNER*

"Wonderful speaker...upbeat and insightful. ...great interaction with the audience." *MANAGEMENT CONFERENCE*

"Your presentation was a hit! Typical comments: "Neat lady"..."Kinza was excellent, ....I thoroughly enjoyed Kinza's presentation"... "I loved 'Hurray, It's Monday!..I really needed that!'." *MEDICAL SERVICES*

"Thank you, Kinza! Your program was well received by all of our bank employees and our branch managers. You made the session fun and very worthwhile—-they are still talking about it as well as the lessons learned. *FINANCIAL INDUSTRY*

"Everyone was struck by your enthusiasm and energy, and a lot of us really identified with the life stories you used. You set the tone for our whole conference. *PROFESSIONAL WOMEN*

"As a tribal nation, we consider planning for seven generations Kinza's excellent presentations skills made the topic fun as she provided relevant and effective information for all.." *TRIBUNAL NATION MEETING*

"Kinza's presentation on image management received a "5" (Best) rating from our 300 attendees. Her grand entrance grabbed their attention and she held it all the way through. They loved it!"

*PROFESSIONAL ASSOCIATION*

"We were looking for 'entertainment with a message.' You accomplished our mission!" *MANUFACTURING COMPANY*

"Your program to our sales people was great. You completely disarmed them, drew them in and held heir attention. Excellent." *SALES ASSOCIATION*

"Your keynote was perfect. You really hit home. We had one district officer turn in his resignation that morning. After hearing you speak, he had a change of heart and withdrew his resignation. (You made the difference.)" *SERVICE CLUB*

"Your presentation received high praise: Great job... Uplifting ... Lot's of fun!...We needed this!" *SCHOOL PERSONNEL*

"Kinza's program was excellent in every way. She exceeded our expectations on all counts. Her warmth and enthusiasm are contagious!" *EMPLOYEE RECOGNITION*

"Your opening keynote on the DISC profiling tool for our 150 attendees was described as: Very dynamic.....Great way to start the day ...Speaker was great...Making it personal was an added bonus...Excellent." *HUMAN RESOURCES*

'This was the best program I've ever been to ...Very entertaining and uplifting..... Beyond fantastic...Bring her back!" *WOMEN'S COMMUNITY WELLNESS EVENT*

"A perfect finale to our Conference. Thank you for your wonderful energy and inspiration!" *HEALTH CARE INDUSTY*

"The returning volunteers from the 9/11 disaster sites all had been through difficult assignments. Your program was just what they needed. It was sensitive, respectful and fun. It gave them permission to laugh again. We will remember your program for a long time to come but it will certainly be hard to ever top it for our next event!" *THE AMERICAN RED CROSS*

# ORDER FORM
## Spreading the JAM to Others...

**Please copy and mail your completed order to:**
Peebles Publishing Unlimited
512 Lac La Belle Drive
Oconomowoc, WI 53066

Please send me _____copies of
**Burnt Toast & Jam** @ $12.95                    $ _____
*(For personalized copies, please include names.)*

Wisconsin residents,  add 5.5 % Sales Tax
($.71 per book)                                   $ _____

Shipping and handling: add $2.50 first book,
$1.10 each additional                             $ _____

Enclosed is my check or money order PAYBLE
TO PEEBLES PUBLISHING UNLIMITED for   $ _____

Send To:

Name_____

Address _____

City _____ State_____

Phone (____)_____ Zip Code _____

Please contact the publisher for quantity discounts at  Peebles Publishing  Unlimited, (262) 567-6317. Thank you for your order!